Easy Composer Series

Mein erster Beethoven
My First Beethoven

Die leichtesten Klavierstücke von
Easiest Piano Works by
Ludwig van Beethoven

Herausgegeben von / Edited by
Wilhelm Ohmen

Coverillustration: Silke Bachmann

ED 22359
ISMN 979-0-001-15903-6

English Edition
ED 22395-1

www.schott-music.com

SCHOTT

Mainz · London · Berlin · Madrid · New York · Paris · Prague · Tokyo · Toronto
© 2016 SCHOTT MUSIC GmbH & Co. KG, Mainz · Printed in Germany

Ludwig van Beethoven
Steckbrief

1770	getauft am 17. Dezember (geboren vermutlich am 16. Dezember) in Bonn, wo schon sein Vater Johann und sein Großvater als Sänger des Kurfürstlichen Hofes wirkten
1778	Musikunterricht beim Vater und erstes Konzert in Köln als Pianist
1781	der Bonner Hoforganist Christian Gottlob Neefe unterrichtet und fördert den außerordentlich begabten Jungen und lässt erste Werke im Druck erscheinen
1784	Beethoven wird Organist und Bratschist im Bonner Hoforchester
1787	kurzer Unterricht bei Wolfgang Amadeus Mozart in Wien
1792	Übersiedlung nach Wien, wo er bis zu seinem Tode lebt. Seine Lehrer sind Haydn, Albrechtsberger und Salieri. Sein wichtigster Schüler wird Carl Czerny
1800	Beginn seiner Schwerhörigkeit, die 1819 zur völligen Taubheit führt. Trotzdem beginnt seine glanzvollste Schaffensperiode als Komponist
1820–1827	der taube Beethoven zieht sich mehr und mehr aus der Öffentlichkeit zurück. Seinen Gemütszustand schildert er im *Heiligenstädter Testament*. Er komponiert Meisterwerke wie die 9. Symphonie, die letzten Streichquartette, die letzten Klaviersonaten und die Missa solemnis
1827	er stirbt nach längerer Krankheit am 26. März in Wien. Einer der Fackelträger des großen Leichenzuges war Franz Schubert

Vorwort

Ludwig van Beethoven war, wie Mozart und Haydn, ein Komponist der Klassik. Sein kompositorisches Schaffen bildet den Höhepunkt und den Abschluss dieser Epoche, weist aber schon auf die Romantik hin. In Wien wird er von einflussreichen Gönnern aus Adelskreisen, darunter Graf Ferdinand von Waldstein, und von seinem Schüler Erzherzog Rudolf von Österreich auf Lebenszeit finanziell gefördert. Er kann als Komponist und Pianist ohne feste Anstellung leben.

Er komponierte u. a. Kammermusiken für verschiedene Besetzungen, Streichquartette, Lieder, die Oper *Fidelio*, die *Missa solemnis*, ein Violinkonzert, neun Symphonien, darunter *Eroica* (Nr. 3), Schicksalssymphonie (Nr. 5), Pastorale (Nr. 6) und die Neunte Symphonie mit dem Schlusschor „Freude schöner Götterfunken". Eine zentrale Stellung in seinem Werk nimmt die Klaviermusik ein mit zahlreichen Einzelstücken, Variationszyklen, 32 Sonaten und 5 Klavierkonzerten.

Zur Ausführung der Stücke

Beethoven arbeitete lange und sehr gewissenhaft an seinen Kompositionen. Von den ersten Eintragungen in sein Skizzenbuch, das er immer bei sich trug, bis zur formvollendeten Ausarbeitung änderte und verbesserte er den Notentext unermüdlich. Seine zahlreichen Vortragsbezeichnungen wie die Phrasierung und vor allem die dynamischen Zeichen, u.a. das *sf* (*sforzato*) also ein plötzliches *Forte*, sollten vom Spieler sehr genau beachtet werden. Unter anderem bietet der vorliegende Band die beiden beliebten Sonatinen (G-Dur und F-Dur), die leichte Sonate in G-Dur op. 49 Nr. 2, das Stück *Für Elise* und den langsamen Satz aus der Mondscheinsonate (op. 27 Nr. 2).

Wilhelm Ohmen

Ludwig van Beethoven
Biography

1770	Christened on 17 December (probably born on 16 December) in Bonn, where his father Johann and his grandfather were singers at the Electoral court
1778	Music lessons with his father; gave his first concert performance as a pianist in Cologne
1781	Christian Gottlob Neefe, court organist in Bonn, taught and encouraged the extraordinarily gifted boy, arranging for his early works to be published
1784	Beethoven joined the court orchestra in Bonn as organist and viola player
1787	briefly had lessons with Wolfgang Amadeus Mozart in Vienna
1792	moved to Vienna, where he lived until his death. His teachers were Haydn, Albrechtsberger and Salieri. His most prominent student was Carl Czerny.
1800	beginning of hearing problems, culminating in complete deafness in 1819. This was nevertheless the beginning of his finest creative period as a composer.
1820–1827	completely deaf, Beethoven retired increasingly from public life. He described his state of mind in the *Heiligenstadt Testament*. He composed masterpieces such as his Ninth Symphony, his late String Quartets, late Piano Sonatas and Missa Solemnis.
1827	after a long illness he died in Vienna on 26 March. One of the torchbearers at his grand funeral procession was Franz Schubert

Preface

Like Mozart and Haydn, Ludwig van Beethoven was a classical composer. His compositions represent the culmination and conclusion of that era, while also pointing the way forward to Romanticism. In Vienna Beethoven was supported financially by influential aristocratic patrons who included Count Ferdinand von Waldstein and the Archduke Rudolf of Austria, who took lessons with him. Thus he was able to live as a composer and pianist without fixed employment.

Among his compositions were chamber works for various combinations of instruments, string quartets, songs, the opera *Fidelio*, the *Missa Solemnis*, a violin concerto, nine symphonies including the *Eroica* (No. 3), the great Fifth Symphony with its Fate motif, the Pastoral Symphony (No. 6) and his Ninth Symphony with its final chorus the Hymn of Joy. Piano music is of central importance in his work with numerous individual pieces, cycles of variations, thirty-two sonatas and five piano concertos.

Performing these pieces

Beethoven worked long and carefully at his compositions. From the first drafts in the notebook he always carried with him to the perfectly crafted final form, he would adjust and improve his compositions tirelessly. His many performance markings relating to phrasing and dynamics, in particular, including *sf (sforzato)* indicating a sudden *forte*, should be closely observed by players. Among other pieces this volume includes the two popular Sonatinas (in G major and F major), the easy Sonata in G major op. 49 No. 2, the piece *Für Elise* and the slow movement from the Moonlight Sonata (op. 27 No. 2).

Wilhelm Ohmen
Translation Julia Rushworth

Inhalt / Contents

Ecossaise Es-Dur / E flat major WoO 86	5
Deutscher Tanz C-Dur / German Dance C major WoO 8	6
Deutscher Tanz F-Dur / German Dance F major WoO 8	7
Deutscher Tanz G-Dur / German Dance G major WoO 8	8
Ländlerischer Tanz / Ländler D major WoO 11/1	9
Ländlerischer Tanz / Ländler D major WoO 11/3	10
Ländlerischer Tanz / Ländler D major WoO 11/5	11
Ländlerischer Tanz / Ländler D major WoO 11/6	12
Ländlerischer Tanz / Ländler D major WoO 15/2	13
Deutscher Tanz A-Dur / German Dance A major WoO 42/4	14
Allemande WoO 81	15
Menuett F-Dur / Minuet F major	16
Lustig – Traurig / Happy – Sad WoO 54	17
Für Elise WoO 59	18

Sonatine G-Dur / G major

I Moderato	22
II Romanze	24

Sonatine F-Dur / F major

I Allegro assai	26
II Rondo	28

Leiche Sonate G-Dur / Easy Sonata G major op. 49/2

I Allegro, ma non troppo	31
II Tempo di Menuetto	36

Sechs Ecossaisen / Six Ecossaises WoO 83	41
Bagatelle D-Dur / D major op. 33/6	46
Bagatelle g-Moll / G minor op. 119/1	49
Sechs Variationen G-Dur / Six Variations G major WoO 70	51
Adagio sostenuto (Mondscheinsonate / Moonlight Sonata) op. 27/2	60

Ecossaise
Es-Dur / E flat major
WoO 86

Ludwig van Beethoven
1770–1827

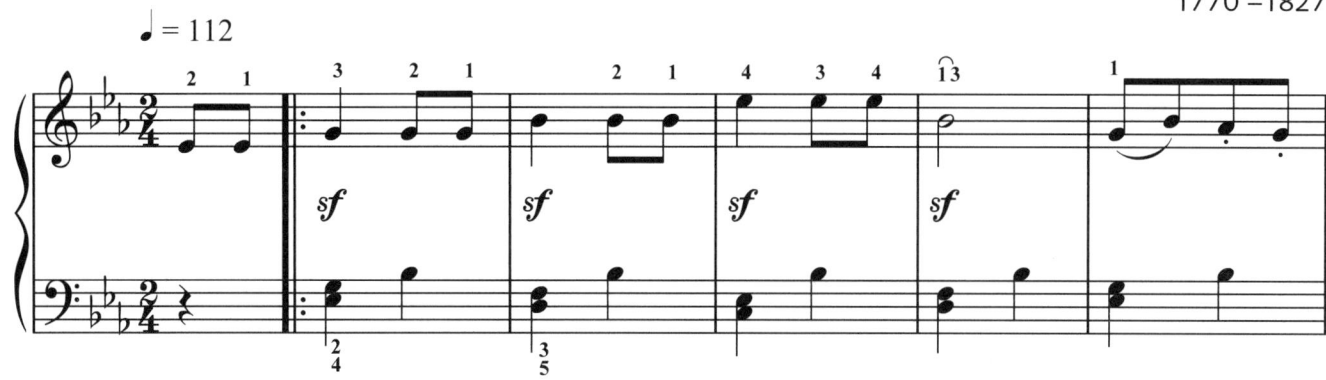

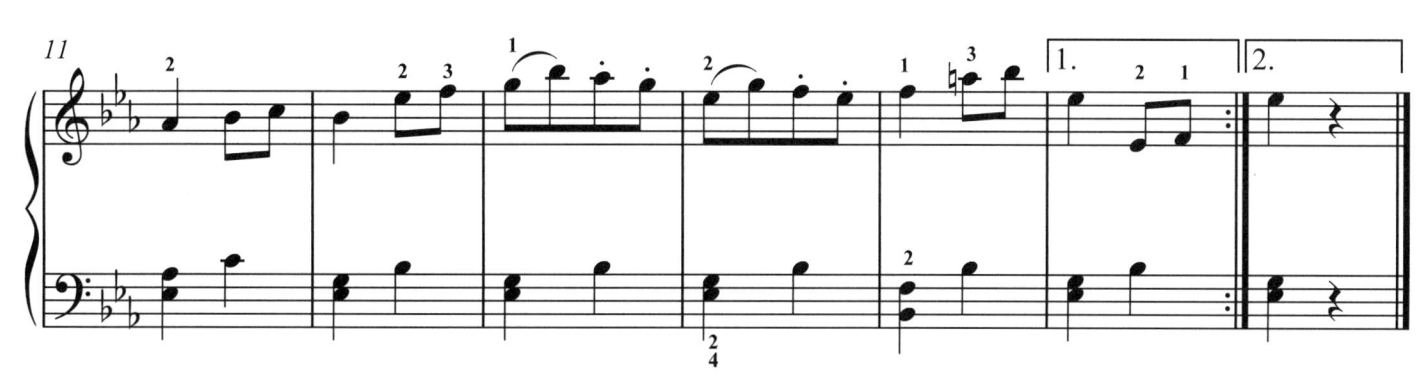

Diese Ecossaise ist eine der letzten Kompositionen für Klavier von L. v. Beethoven.
This Ecossaise is one of the last compositions for piano by L. v. Beethoven.

Deutscher Tanz / German Dance
C-Dur / C major
WoO 8

Ludwig van Beethoven

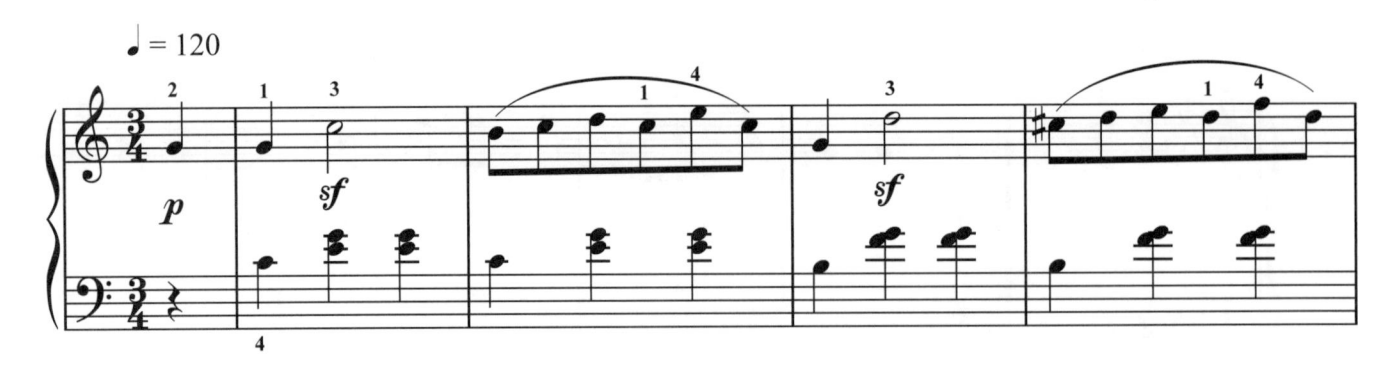

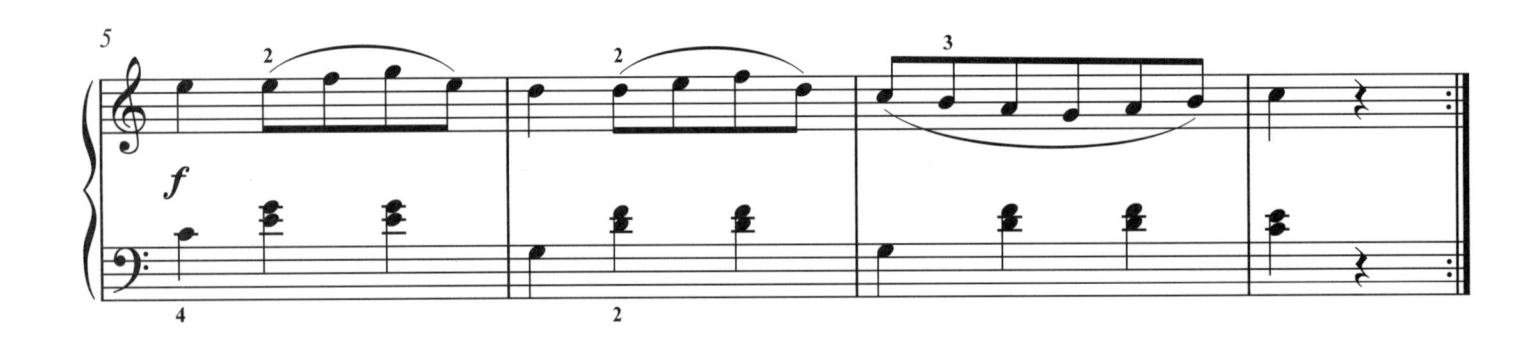

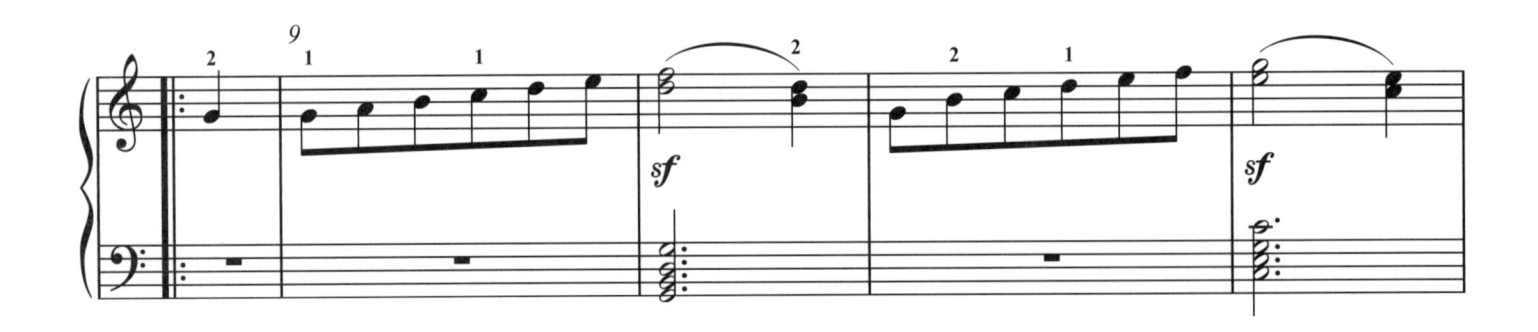

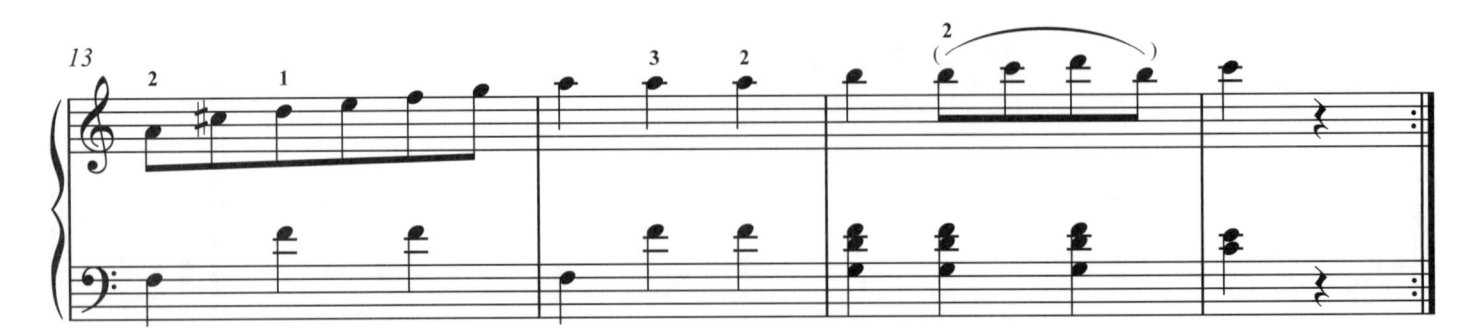

Dieser und die nachfolgendenTänze sind Klavierbearbeitungen von Orchestertänzen, die mit großer Wahrscheinlichkeit von L. v. Beethoven selbst stammen.
This and the following dances are piano arrangements Taf dances for orchestra, which are likely attributed to Beethoven himself.

Deutscher Tanz / German Dance
F-Dur / F major
WoO 8

Ludwig van Beethoven

Deutscher Tanz / German Dance
G-Dur / G major
WoO 8

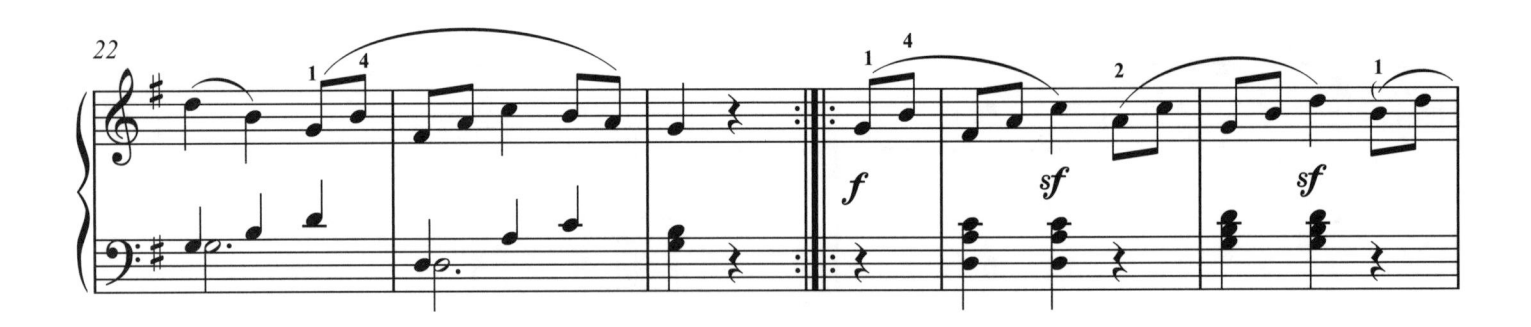

Ludwig van Beethoven

Trio

D. C. al Fine

Ländlerischer Tanz / Ländler
D-Dur / D major
WoO 11/1

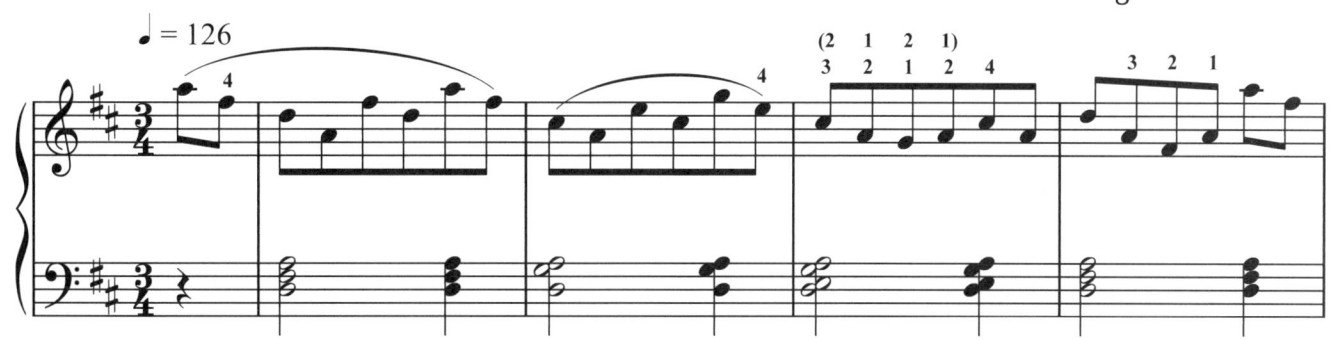

Ludwig van Beethoven

Ländlerischer Tanz / Ländler

D-Dur / D major
WoO 11/3

Ludwig van Beethoven

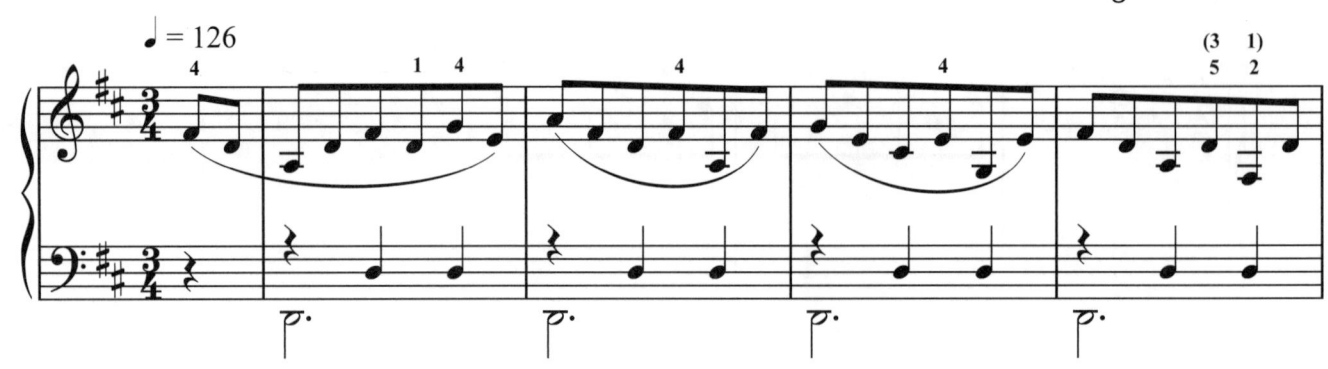

Ländlerischer Tanz / Ländler
D-Dur / D major
WoO 11/5

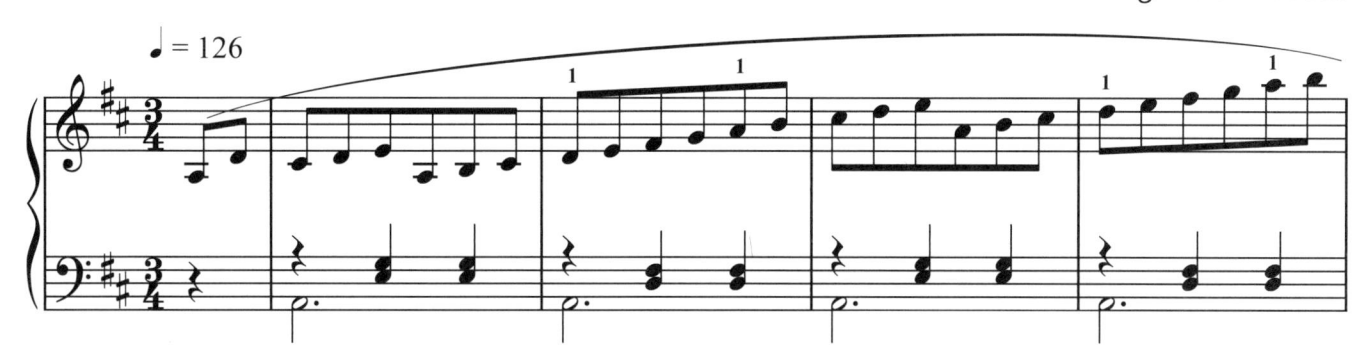

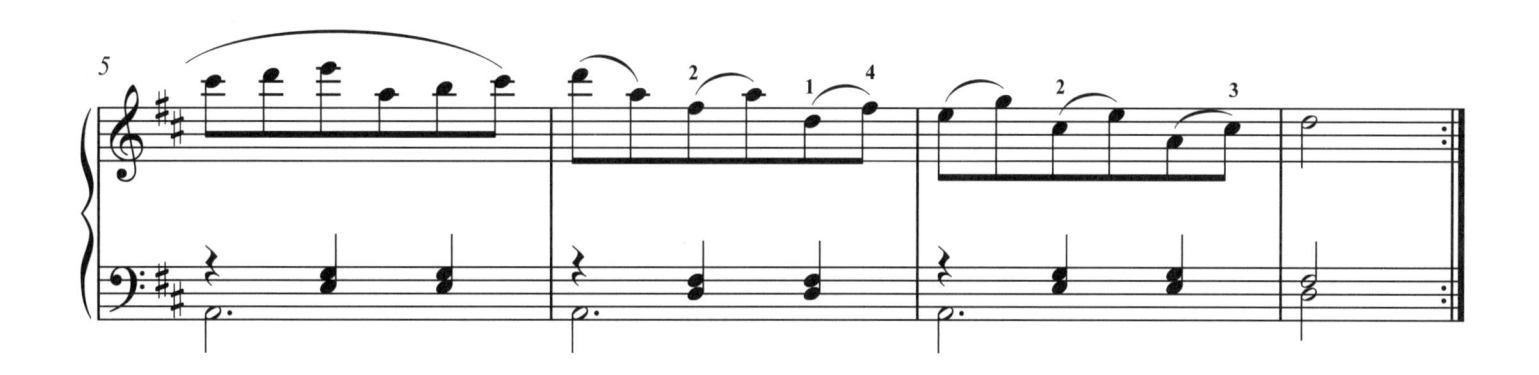

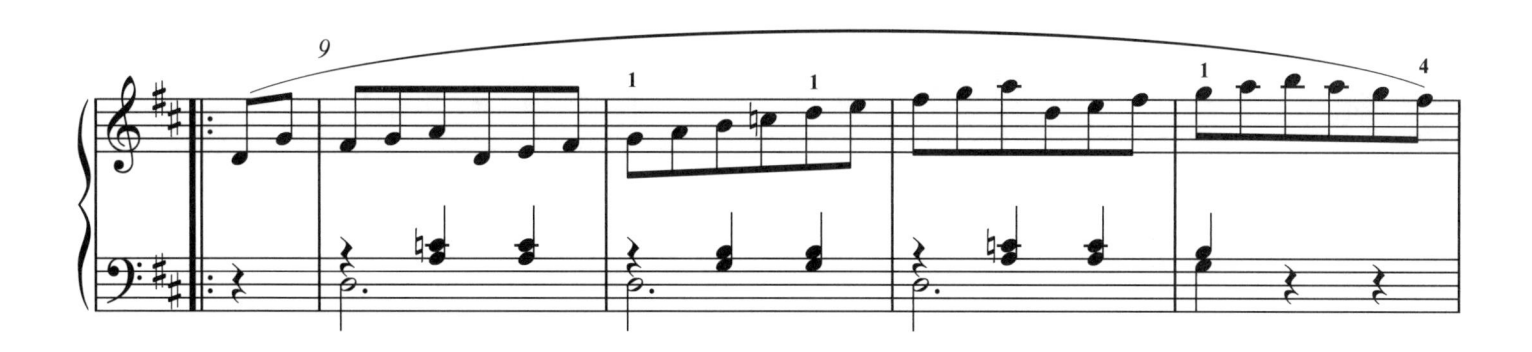

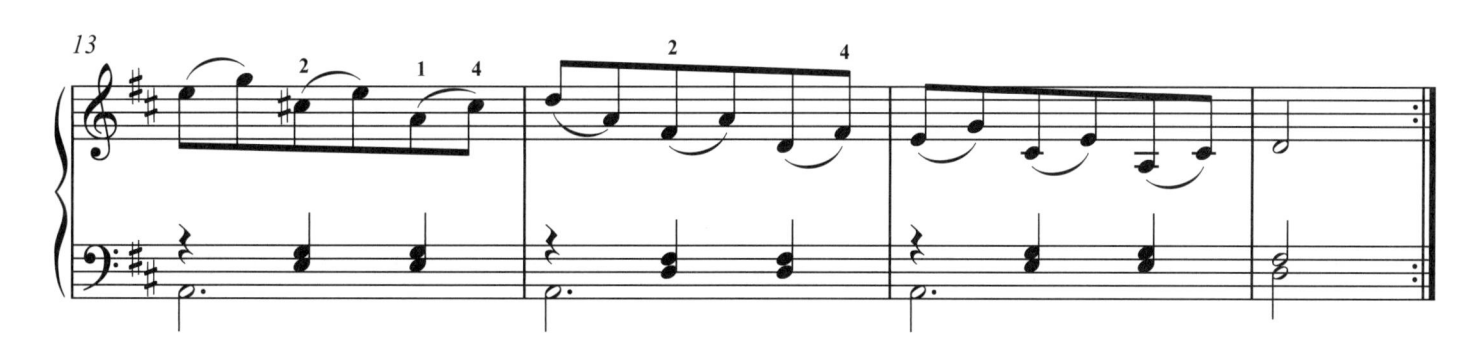

Ludwig van Beethoven

© 2016 Schott Music GmbH & Co. KG, Mainz
aus / from: L. v. Beethoven, 7 Ländlerische Tänze / 7 Ländler, WoO 11

Ländlerischer Tanz / Ländler

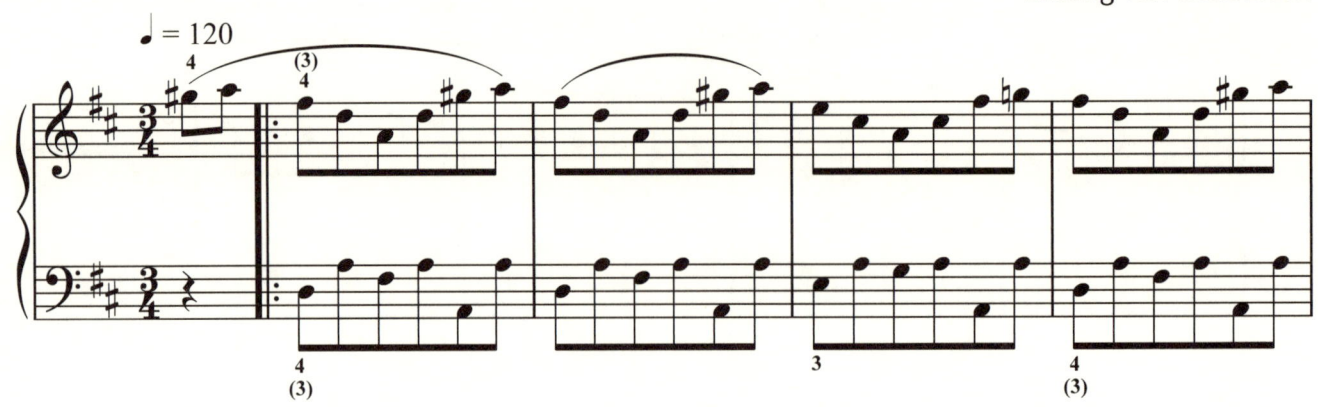

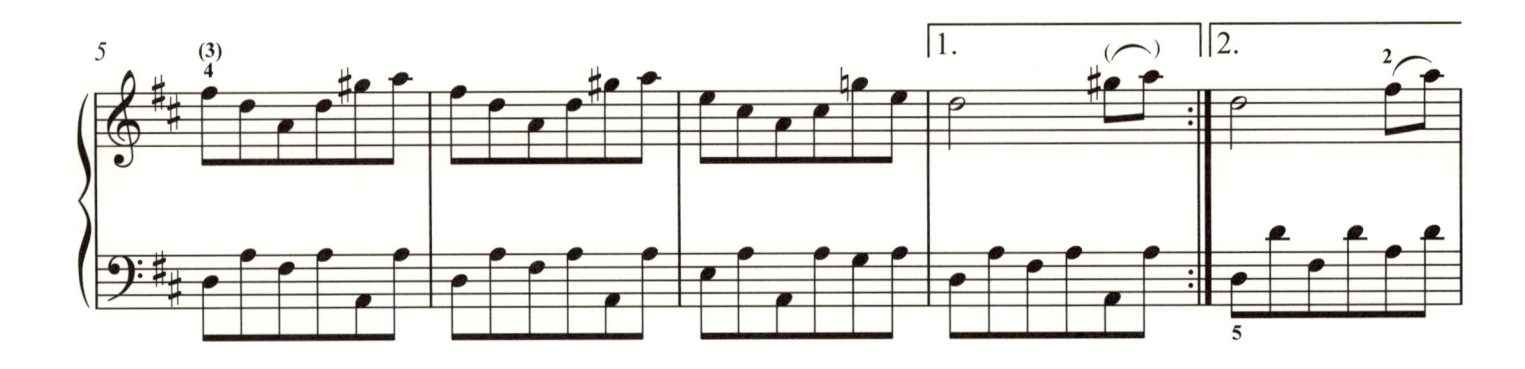

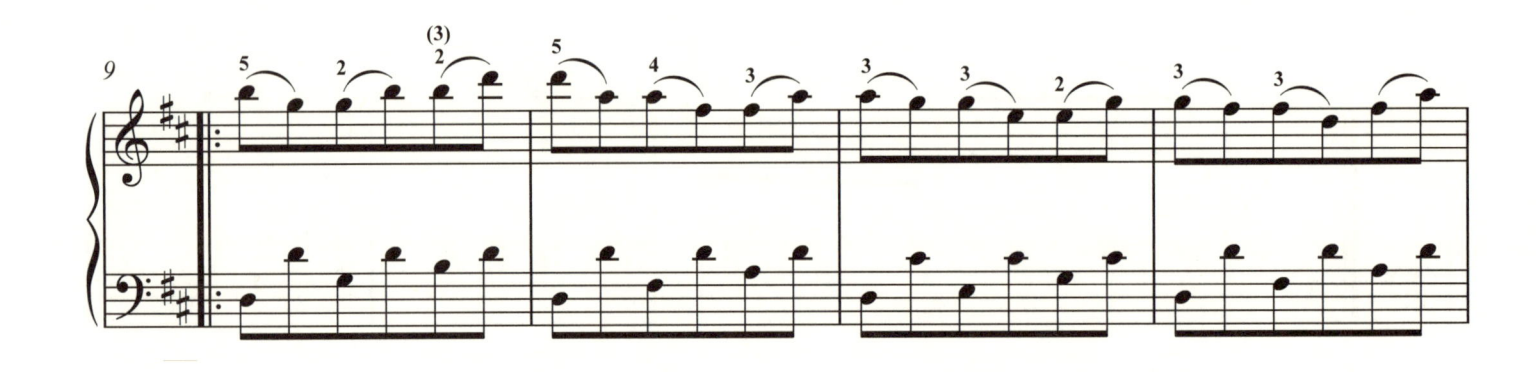

D-Dur / D major
WoO 11/6

Ludwig van Beethoven

Ländlerischer Tanz / Ländler
D-Dur / D major
WoO 15/2

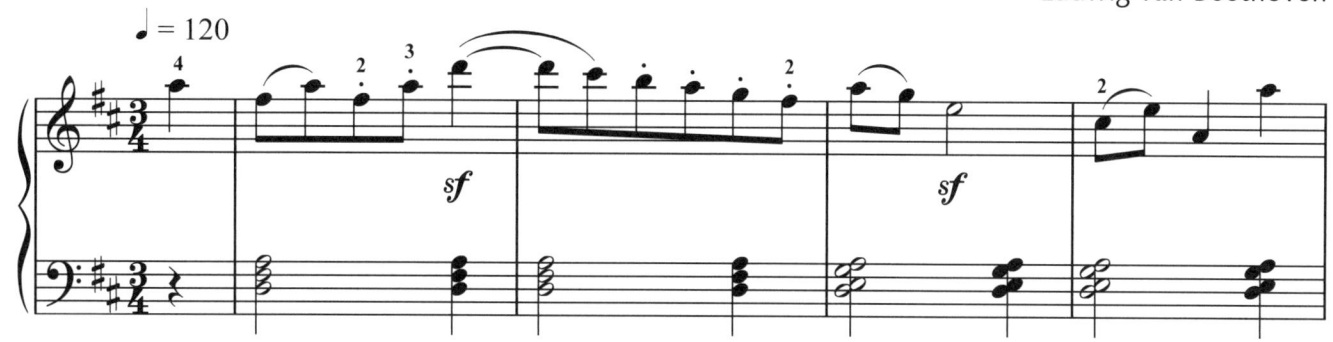

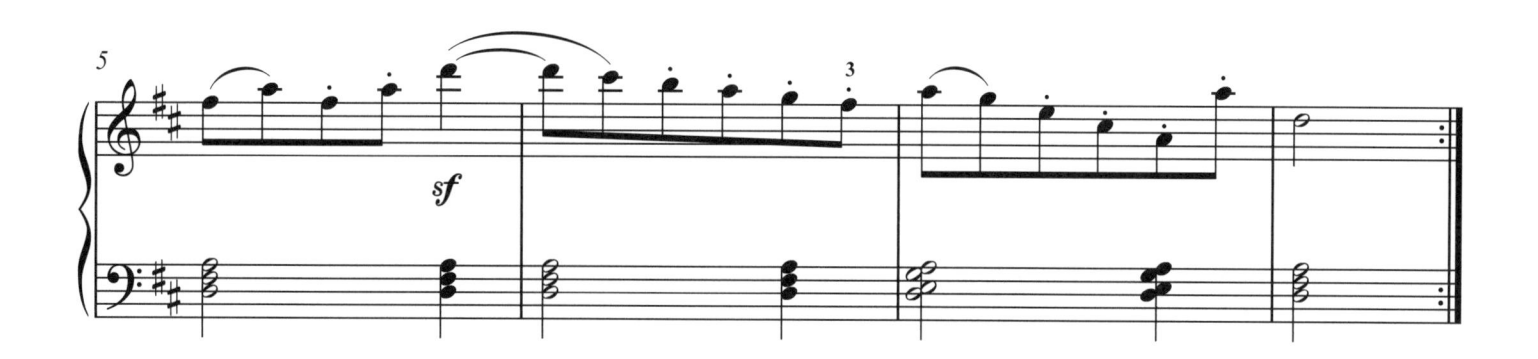

Ludwig van Beethoven

Deutscher Tanz / German Dance
A-Dur / A major
WoO 42/4

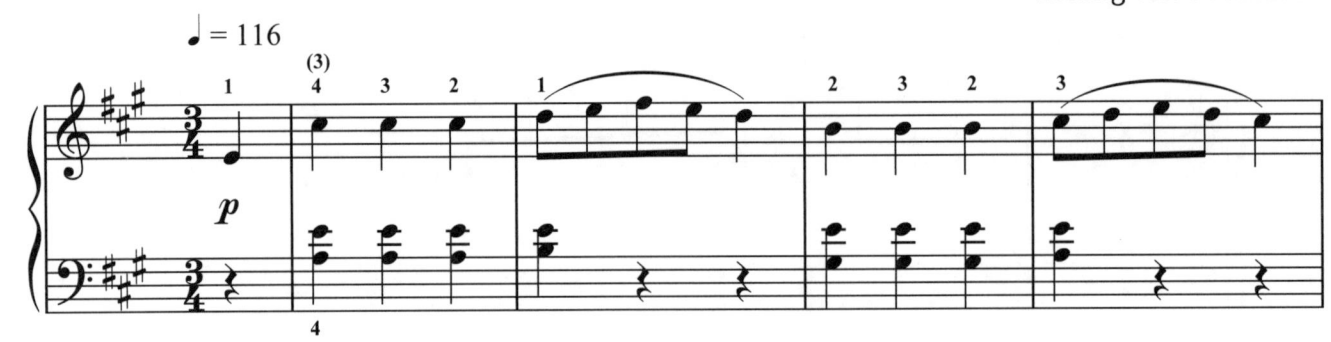

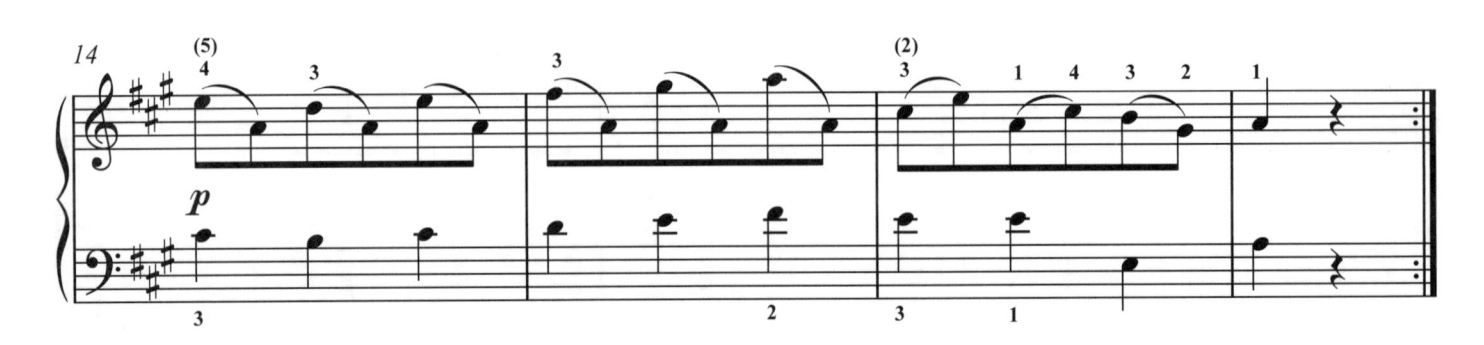

Ludwig van Beethoven

Allemande
WoO 81

Ludwig van Beethoven

Menuett / Minuet
F-Dur / F major

Ludwig van Beethoven

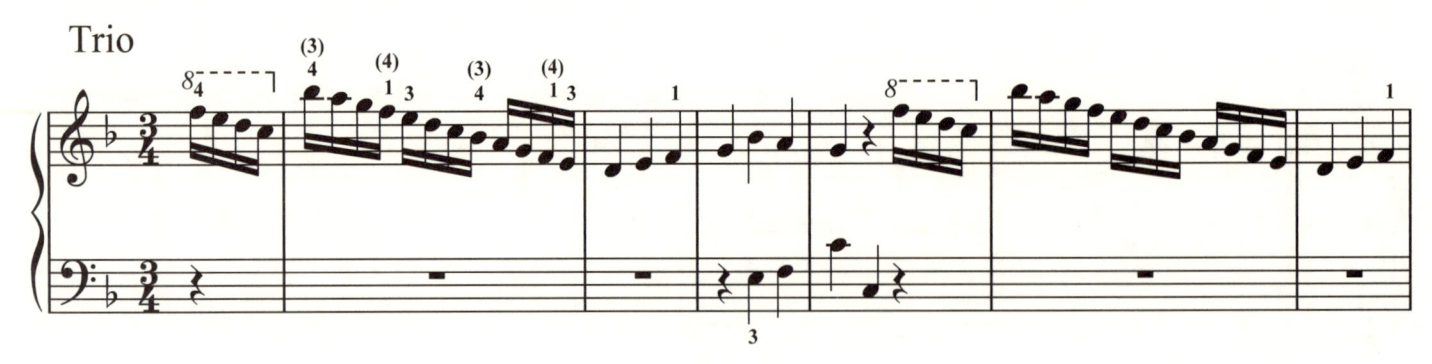

Lustig / Traurig
Happy / Sad
WoO 54

Ludwig van Beethoven

Für Elise
WoO 59

Ludwig van Beethoven

19

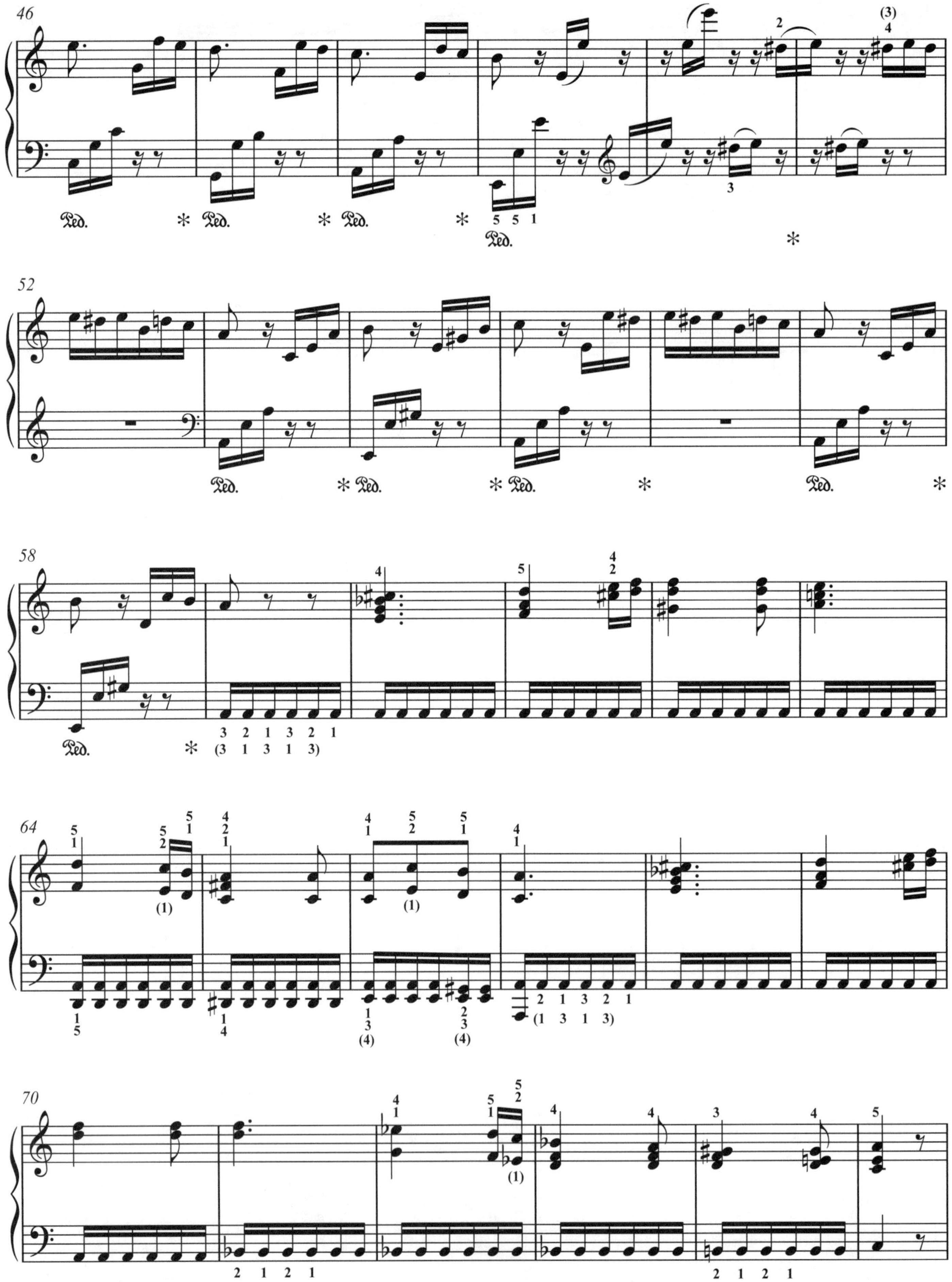
46
52
58
64
70
Ped.

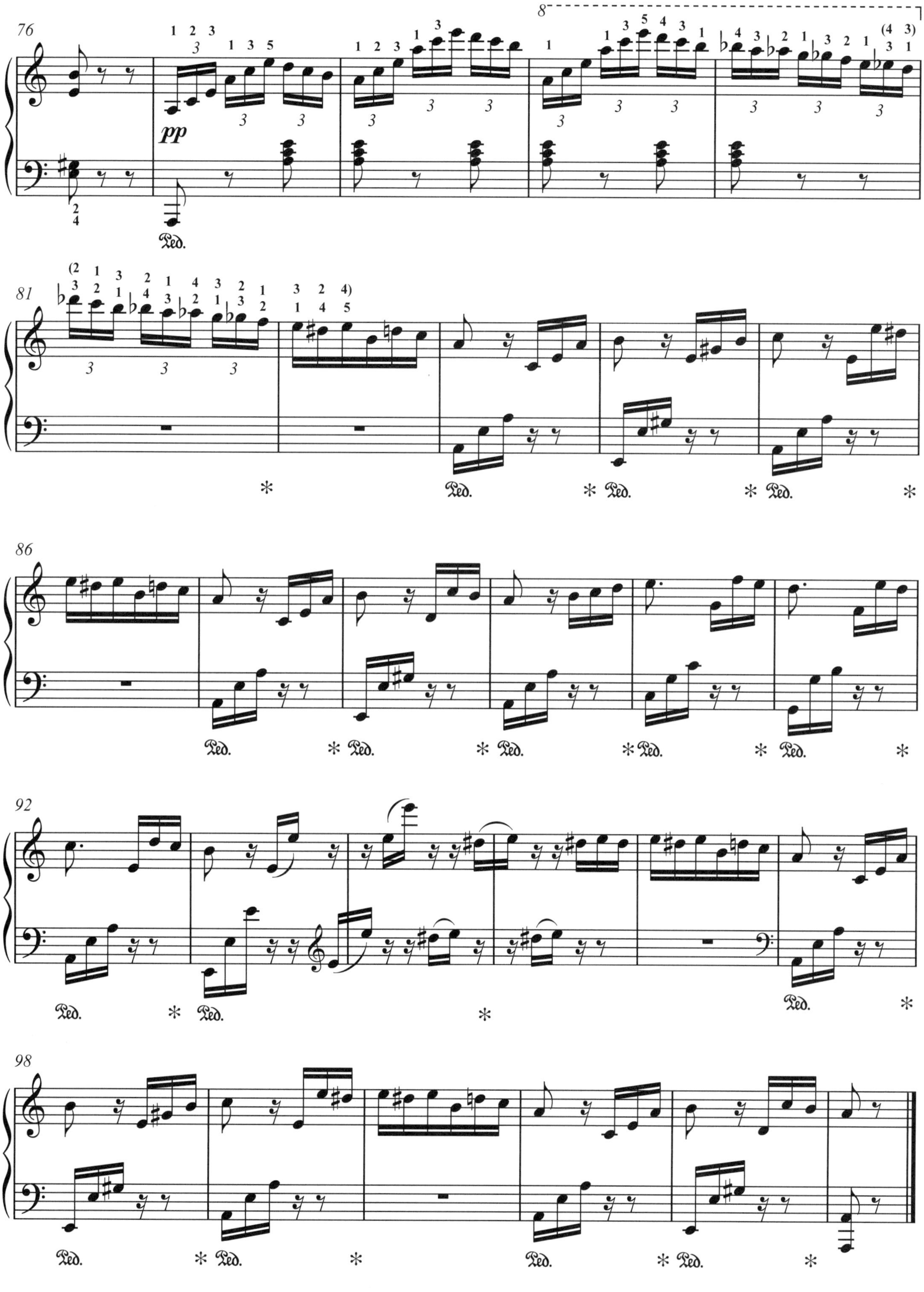
76
pp
Ped.
81
86
92
98

Sonatine
G-Dur / G major

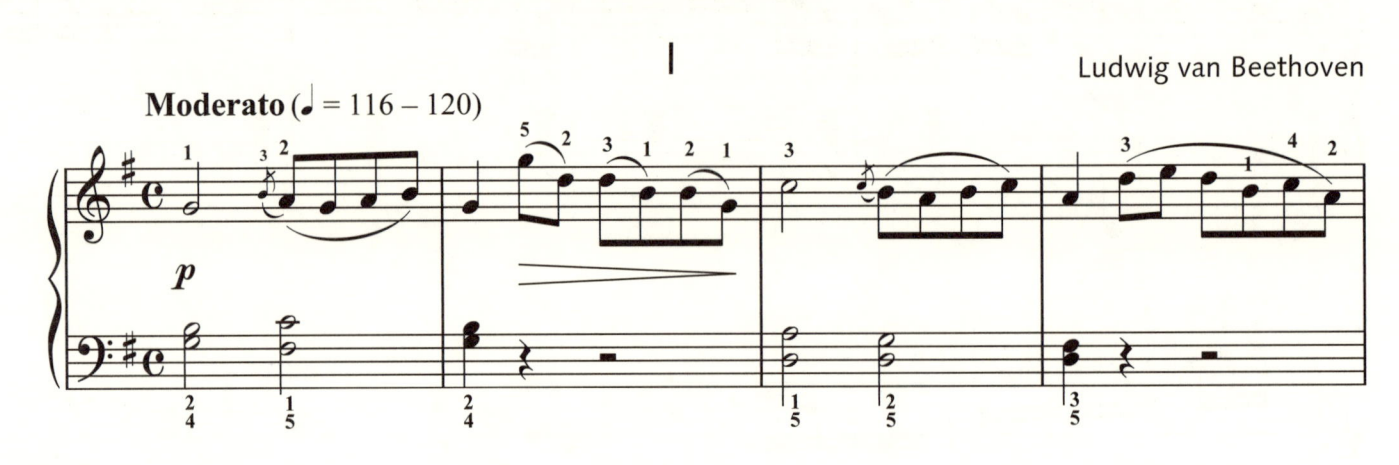

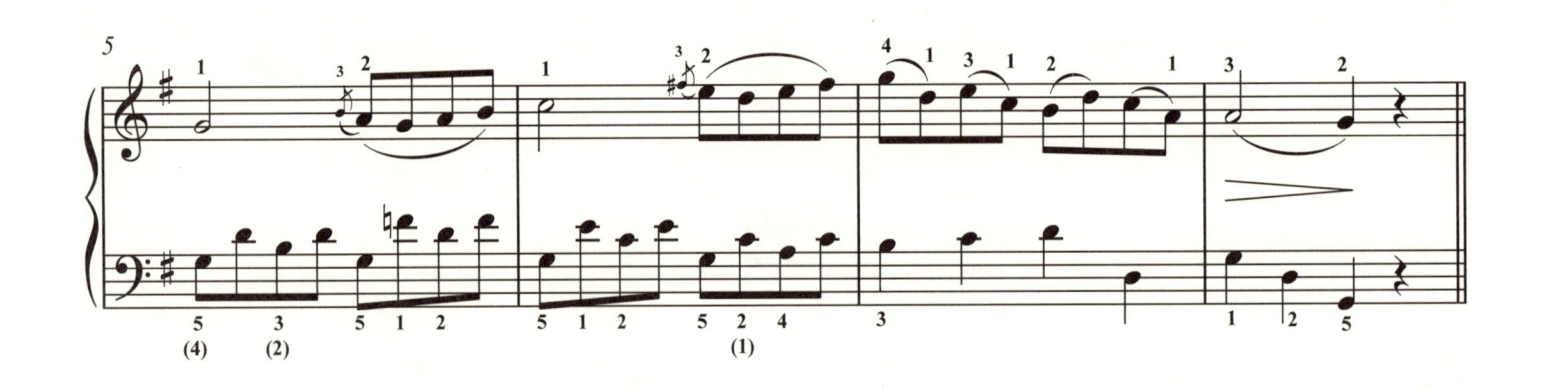

I

Ludwig van Beethoven

Moderato (♩ = 116 – 120)

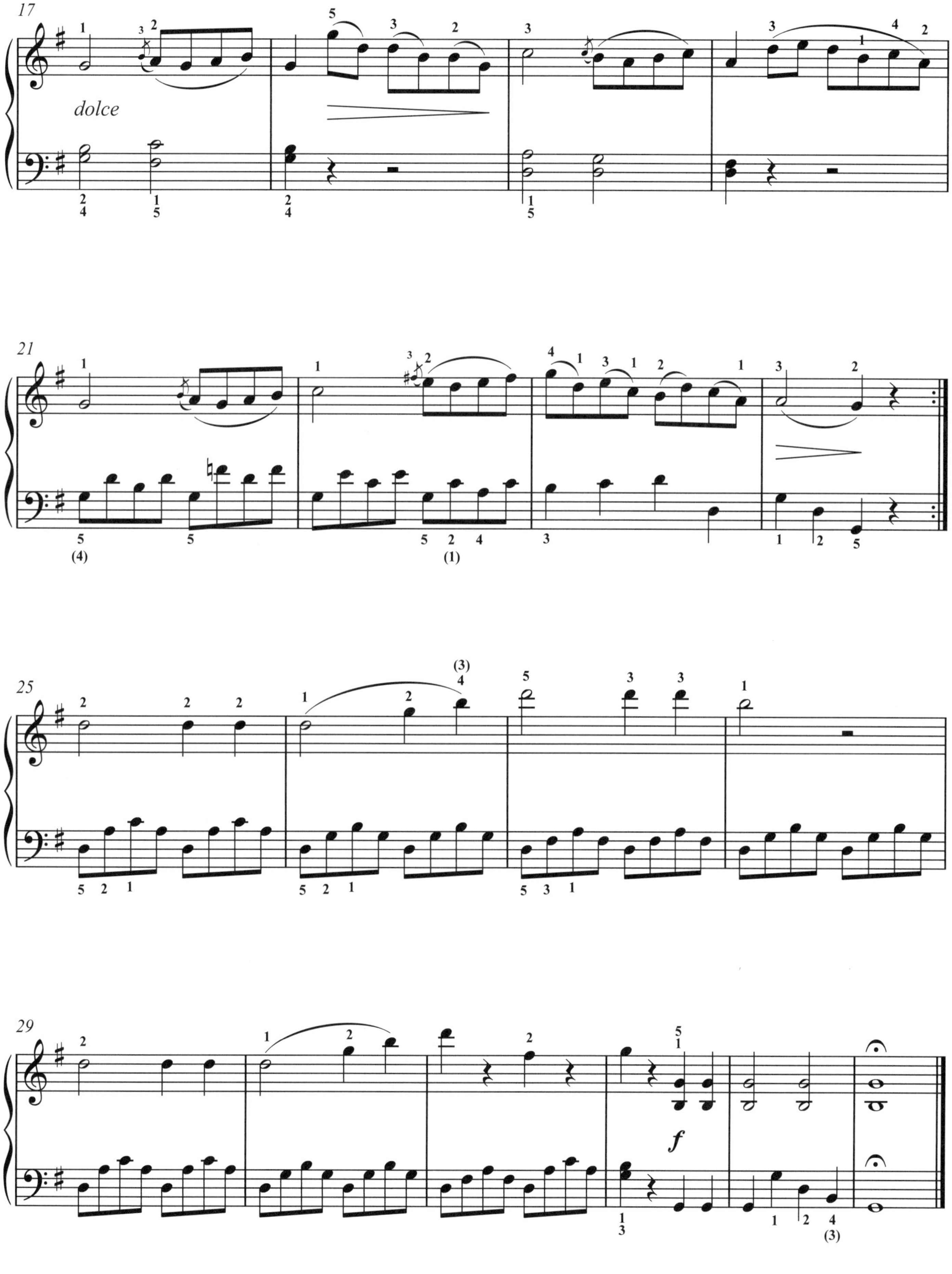
17
dolce
21
25
29
f

II

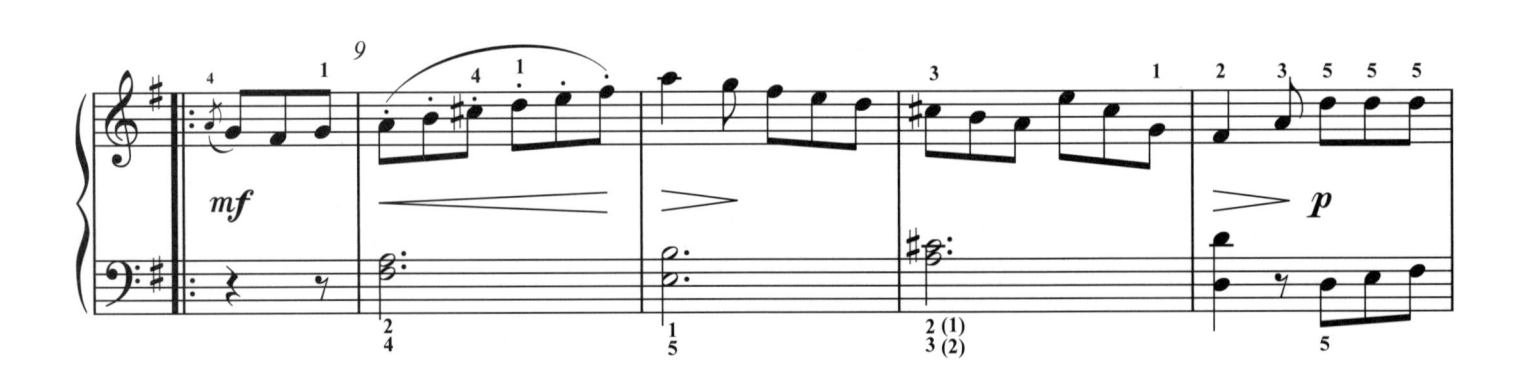

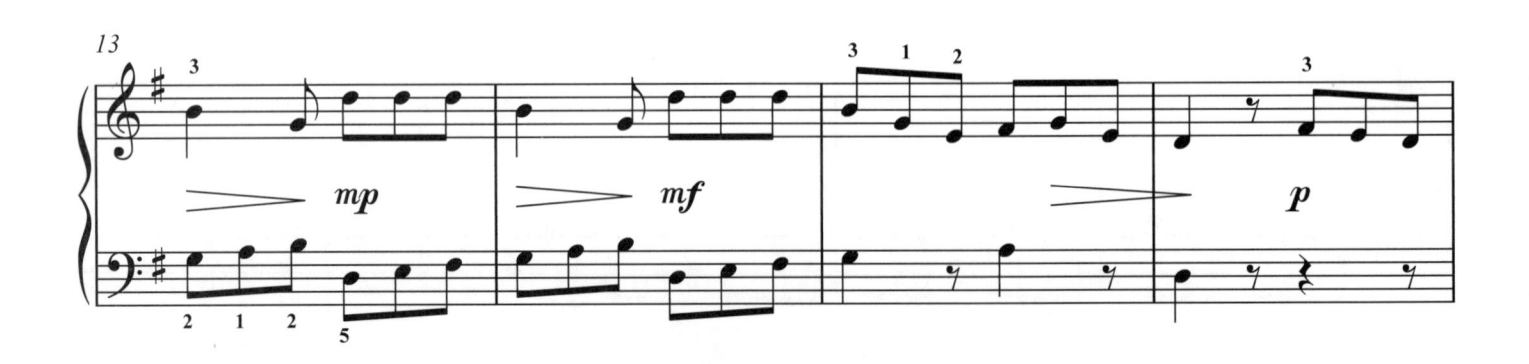

Ludwig van Beethoven

Romanze (♩. = 72 – 76)

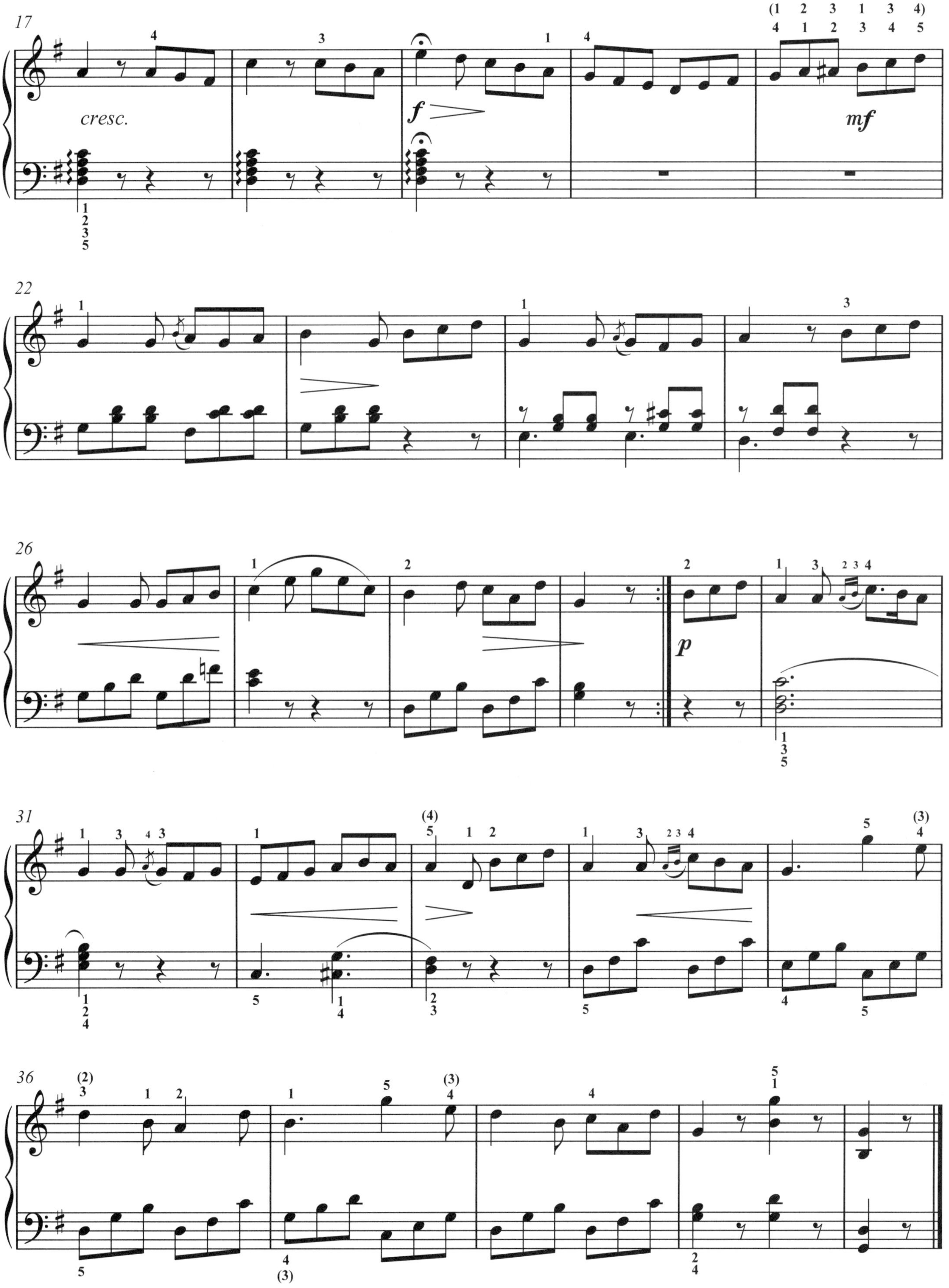
17
cresc.
f
mf
22
26
p
31
36

Sonatine
F-Dur / F major

Ludwig van Beethoven

I

Allegro assai (♩ = 80)

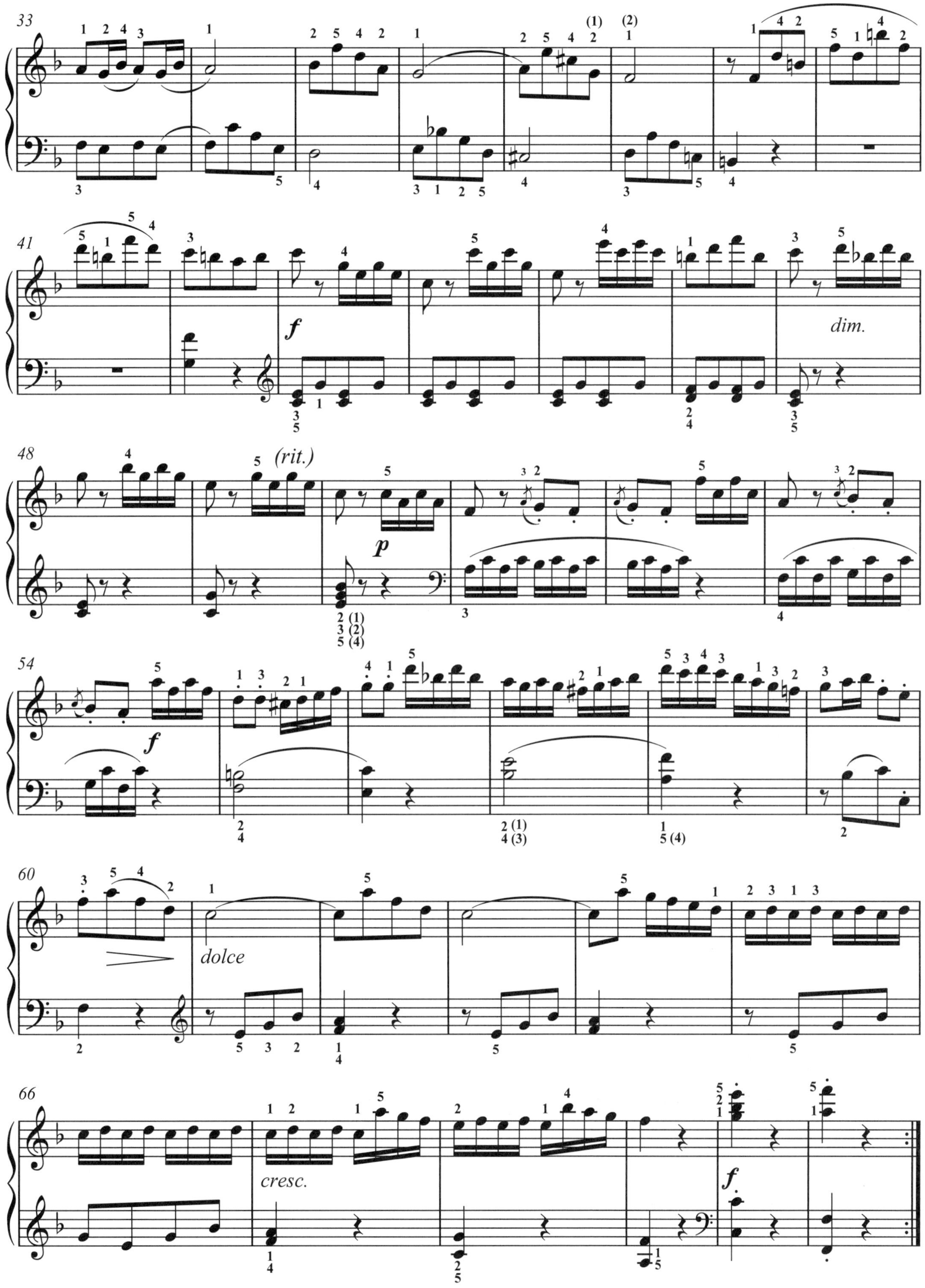
dim.
(rit.)
dolce
cresc.

II
Rondo

Ludwig van Beethoven

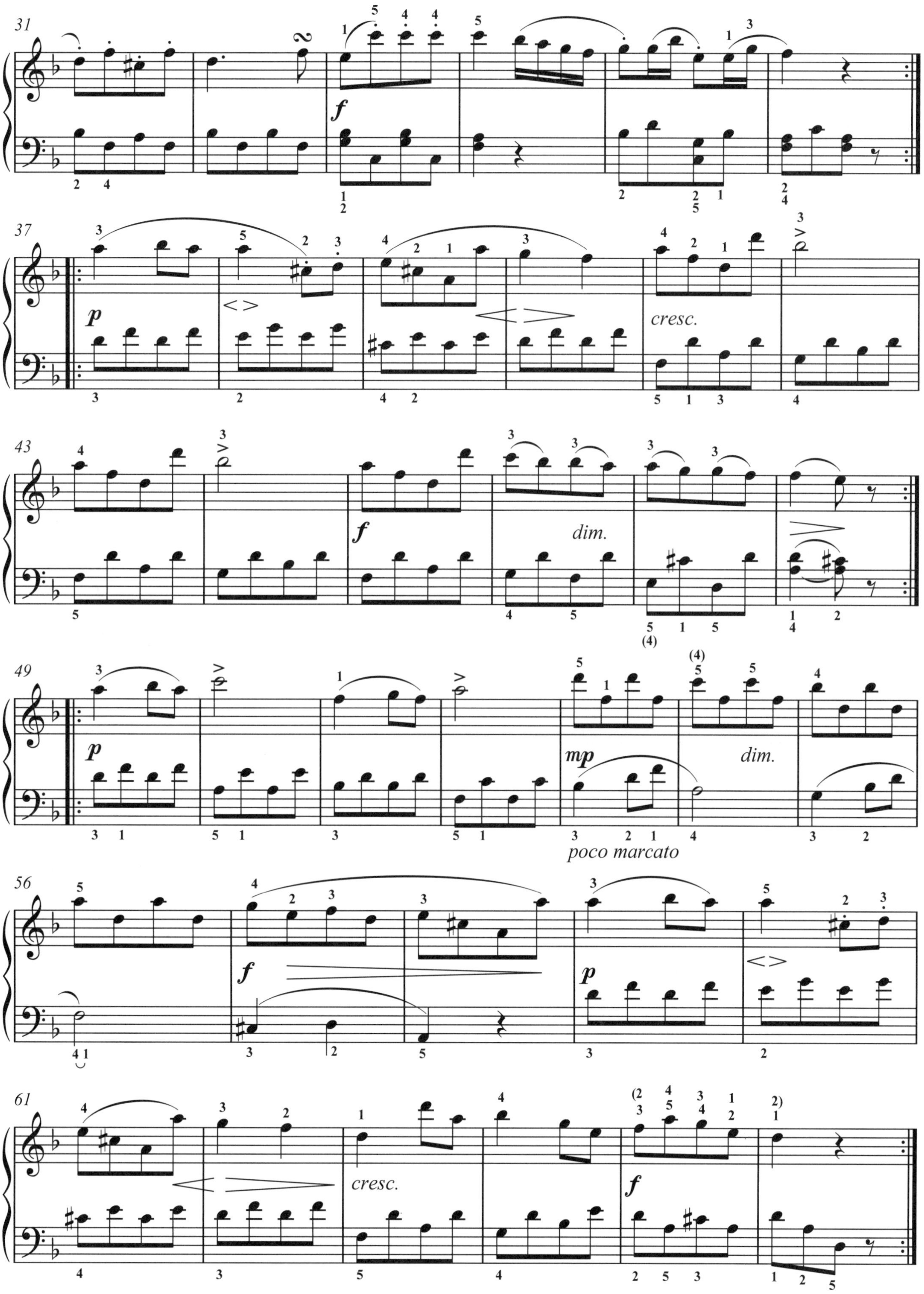
cresc.
dim.
poco marcato
dim.
cresc.

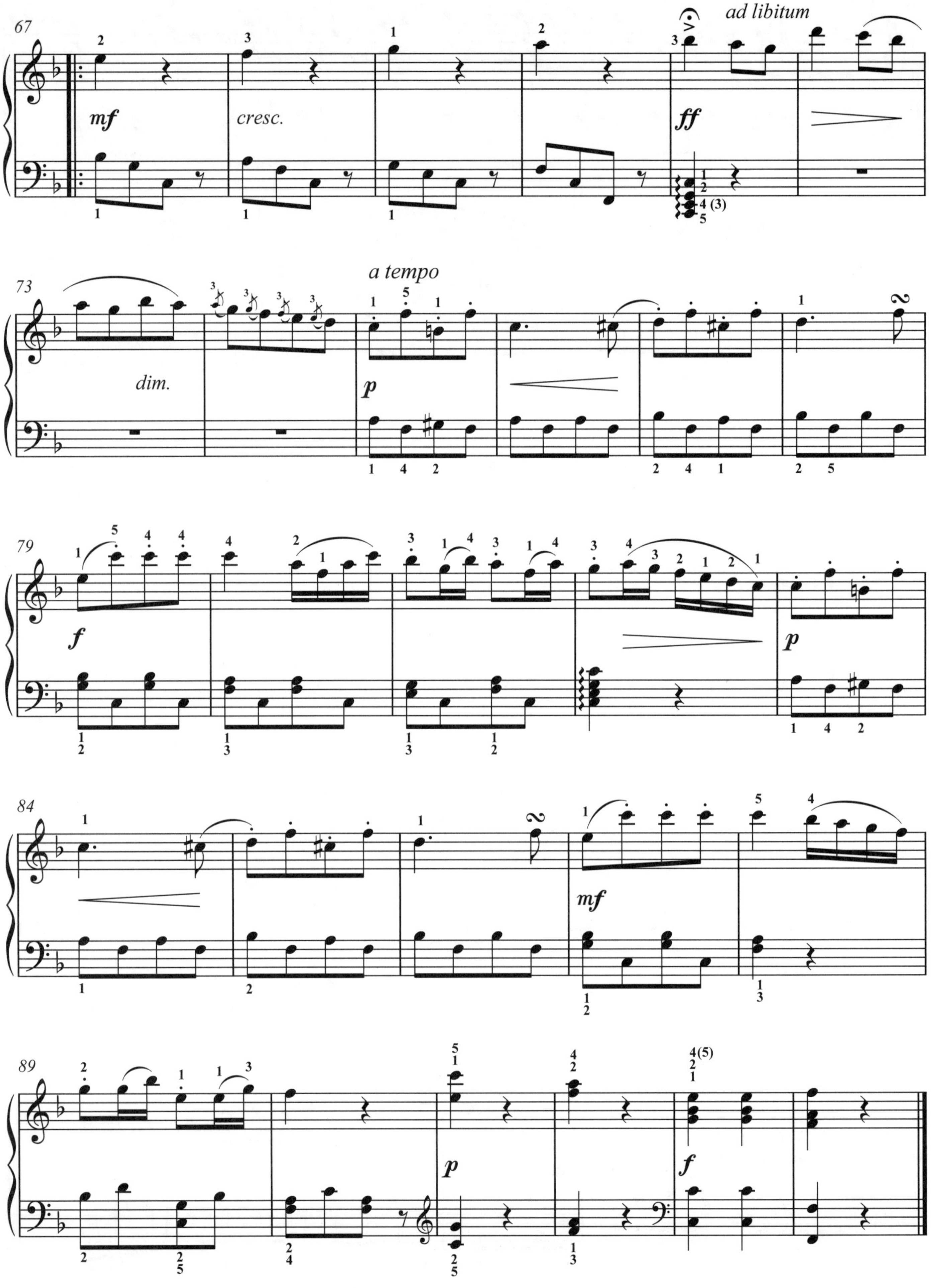
67
ad libitum
mf
cresc.
ff
73
a tempo
dim.
p
79
f
p
84
mf
89
p
f

Leichte Sonate / Easy Sonata
G-Dur / G major
op. 49/2

Ludwig van Beethoven

Allegro, ma non troppo (♩ = 126)

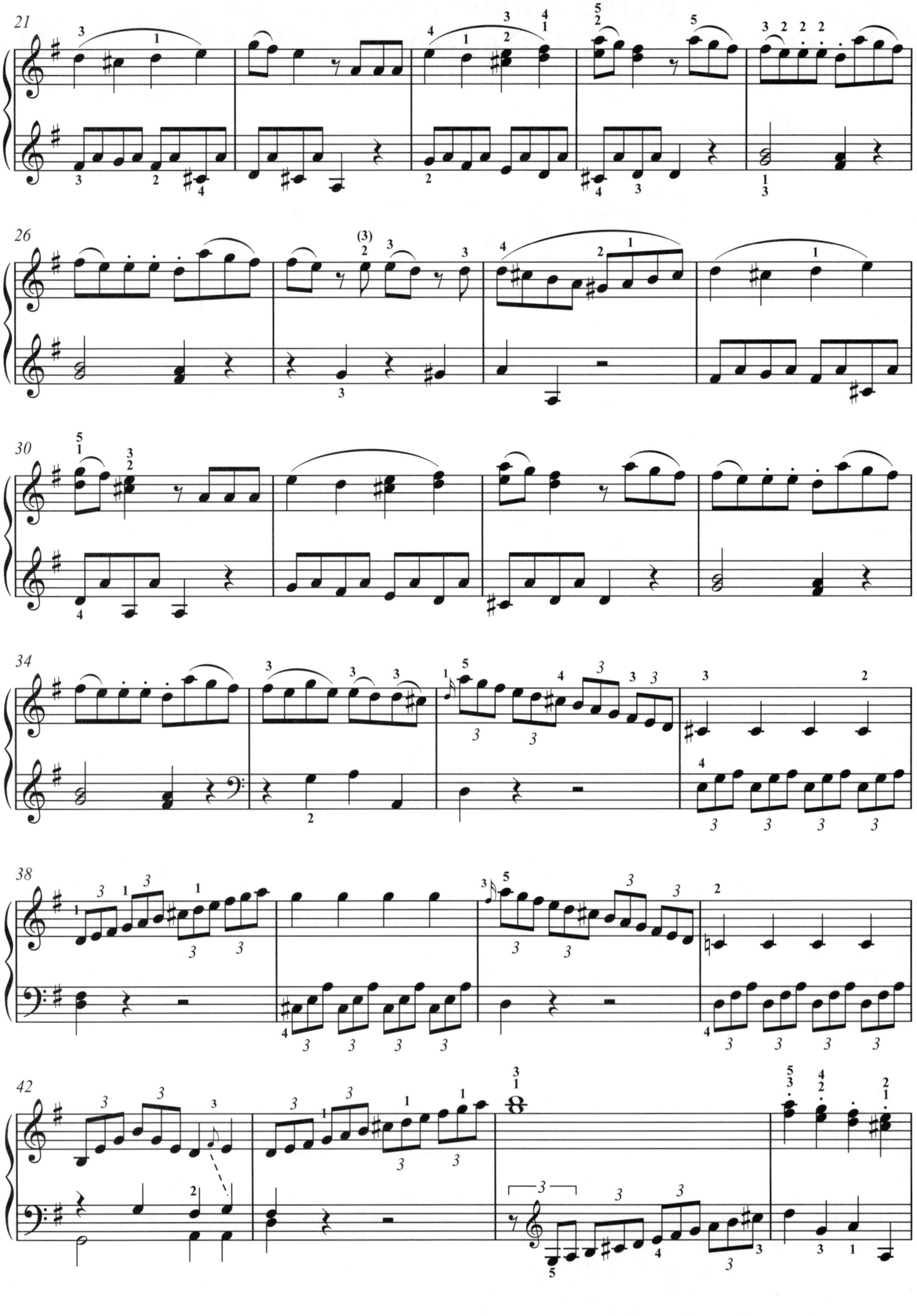
21
26
30
34
38
42

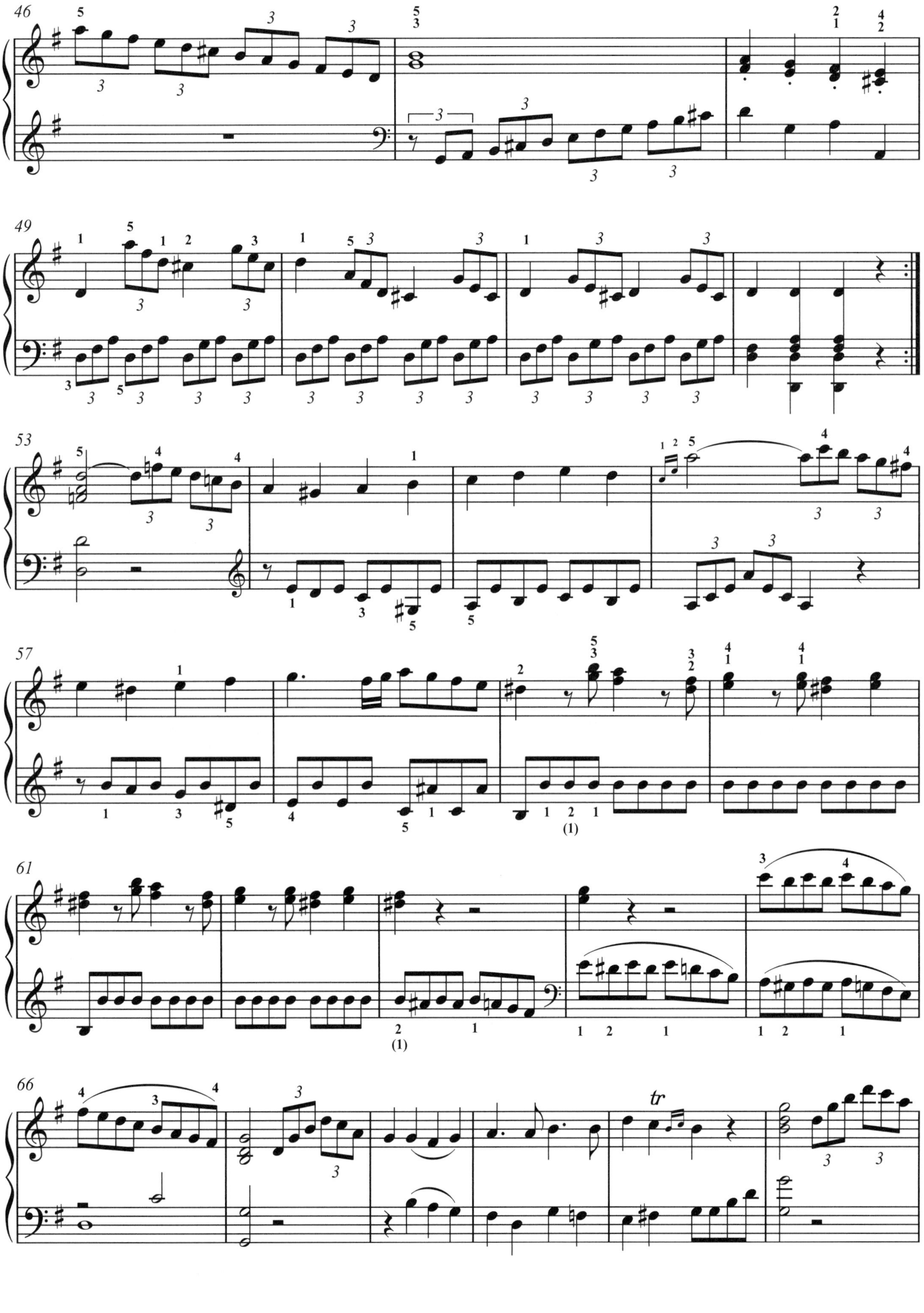
46
49
53
57
61
66
tr

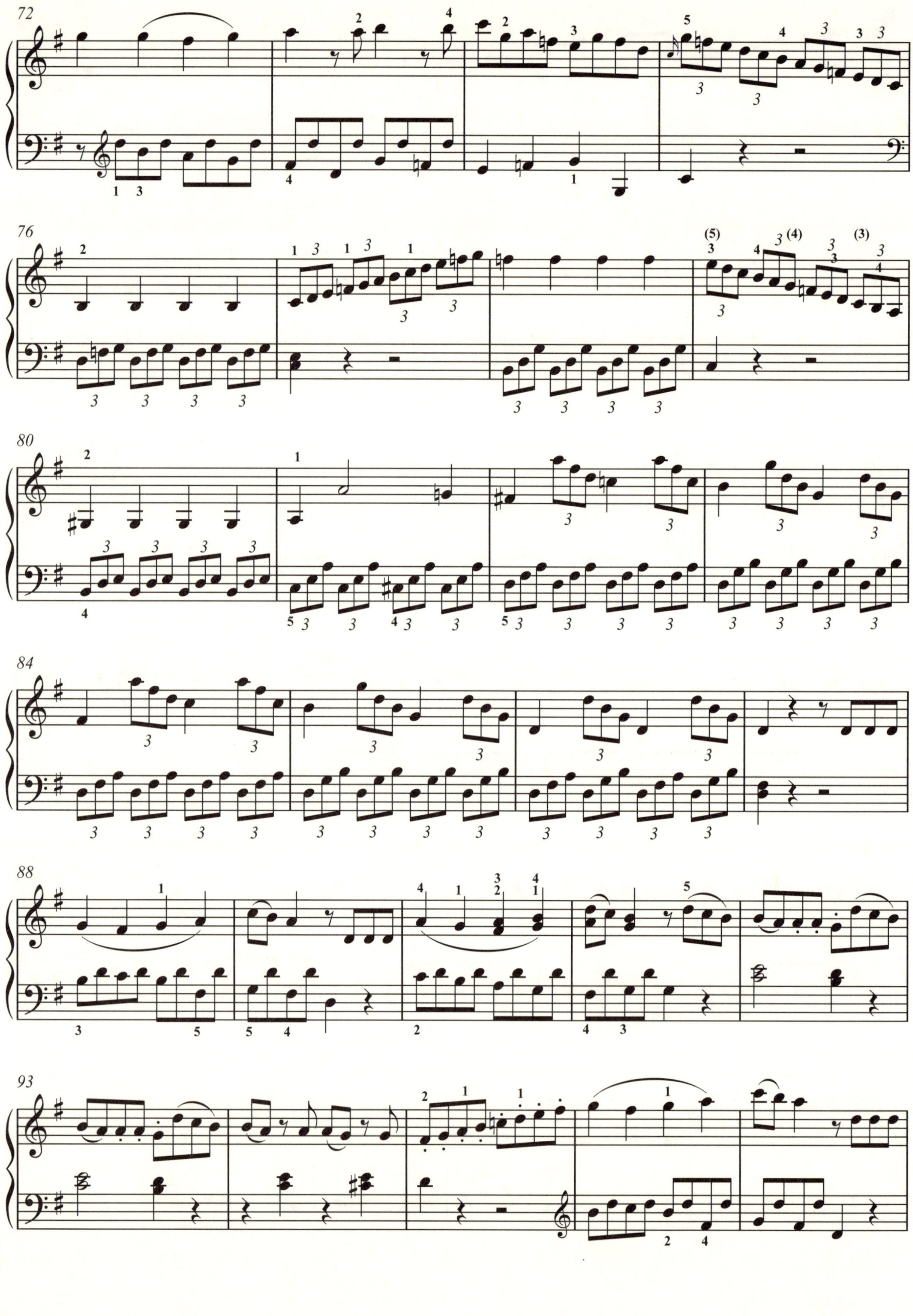
72
76
80
84
88
93

35

II

Tempo di Menuetto (♩ = 104)

Ludwig van Beethoven

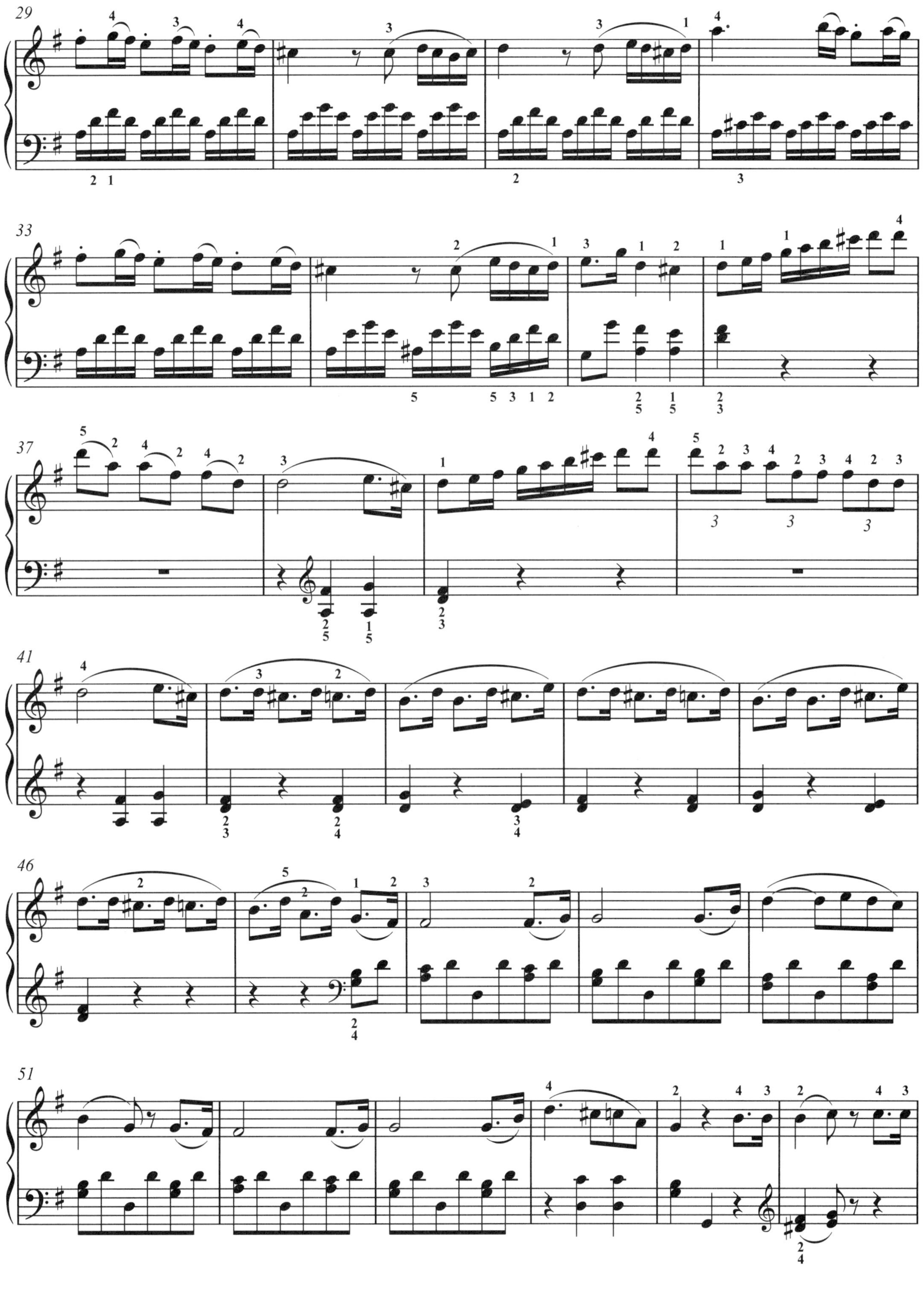
29
33
37
41
46
51

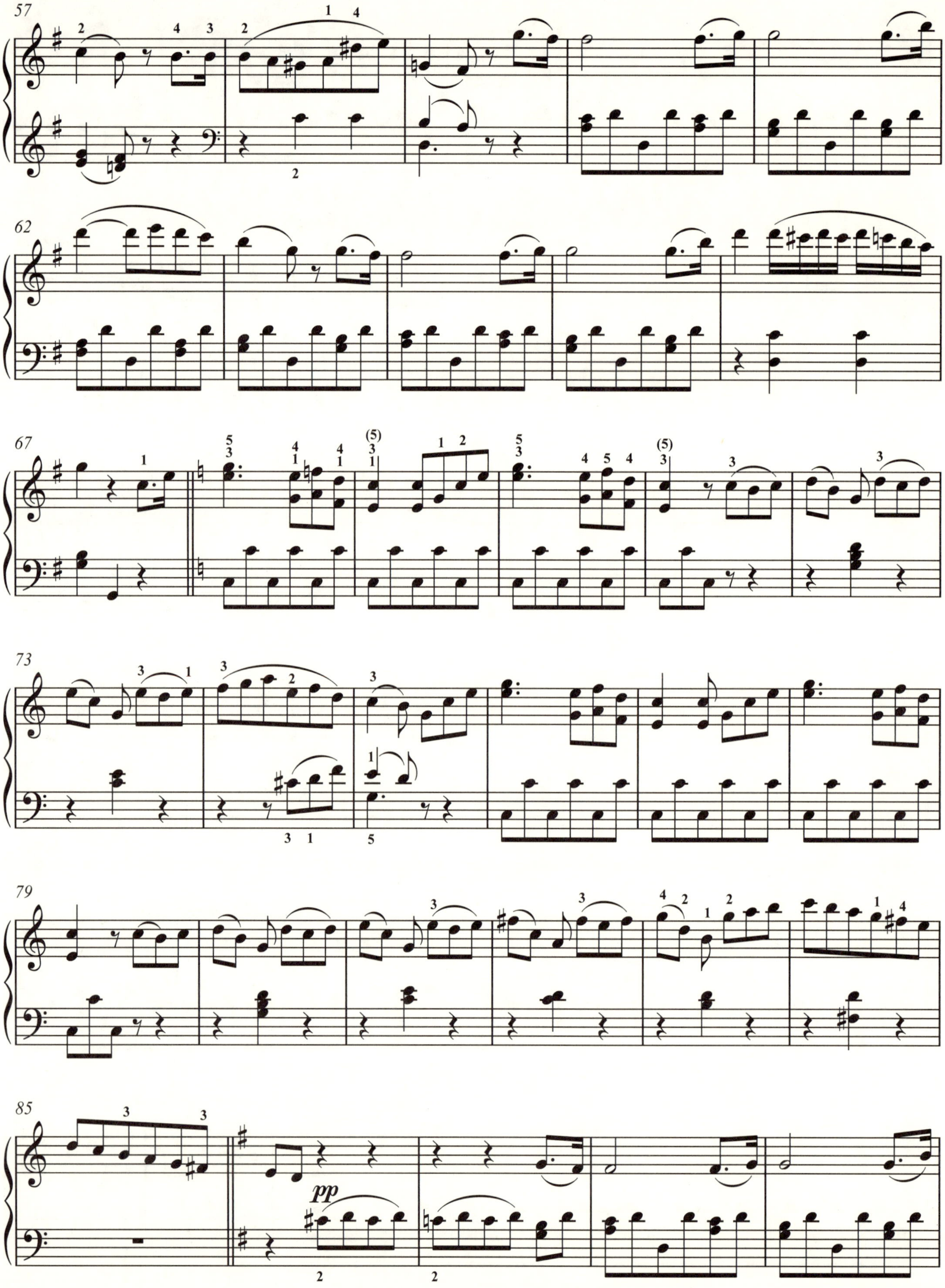
57
62
67
73
79
85
pp

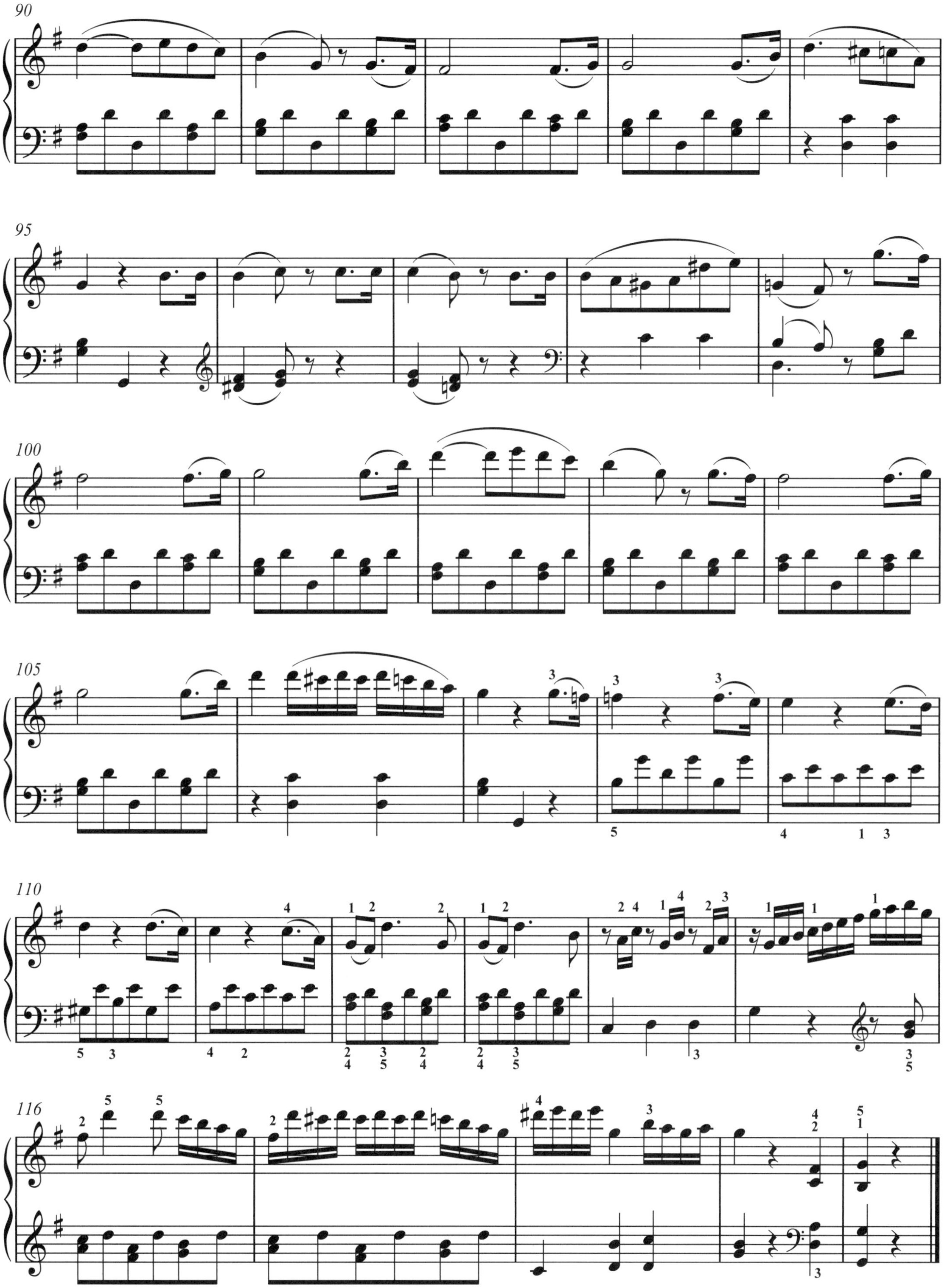
90
95
100
105
110
116

Aus wendetechnischen Gründen bleibt diese Seite frei
This page is left blank to save an unnecessary page turn.

Sechs Ecossaisen / Six Ecossaises
WoO 83

Ludwig van Beethoven

42

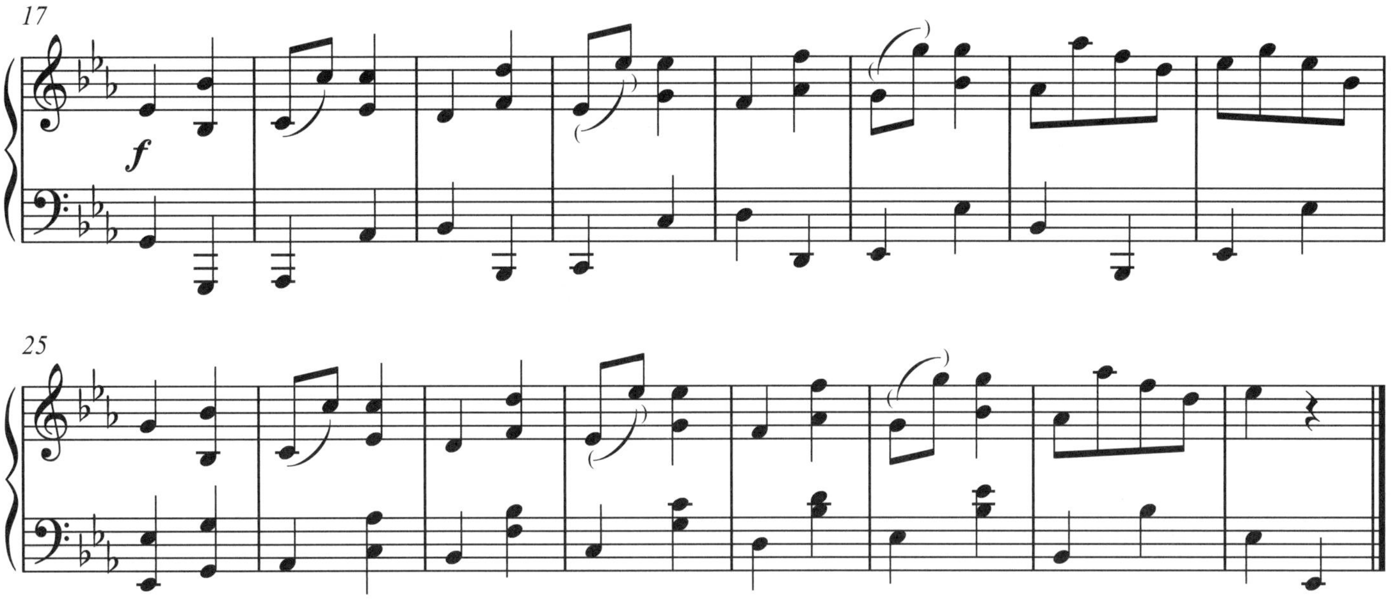

4

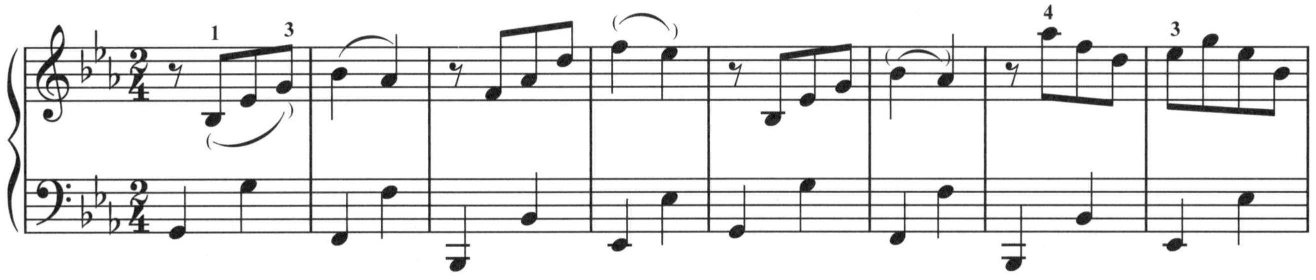

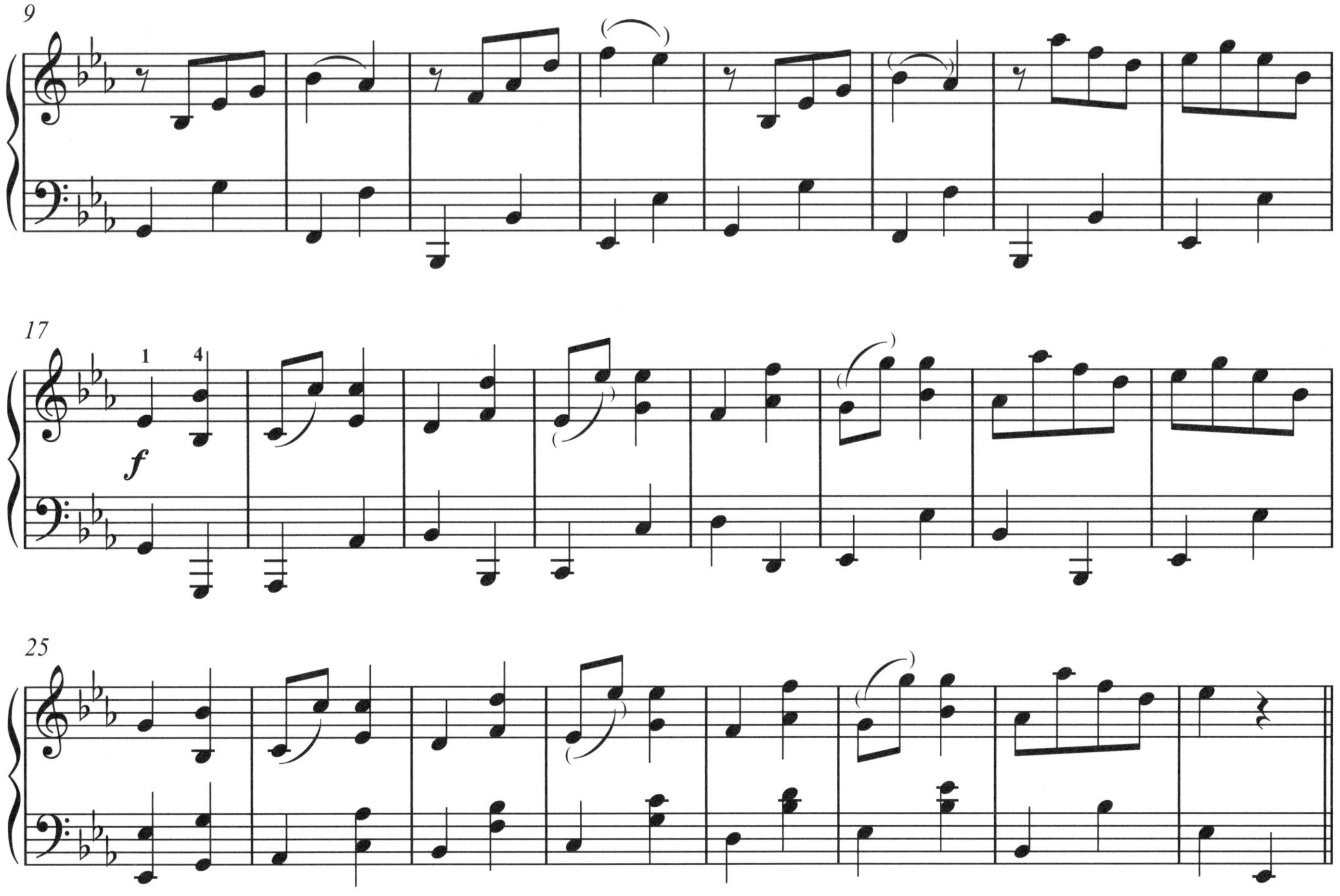

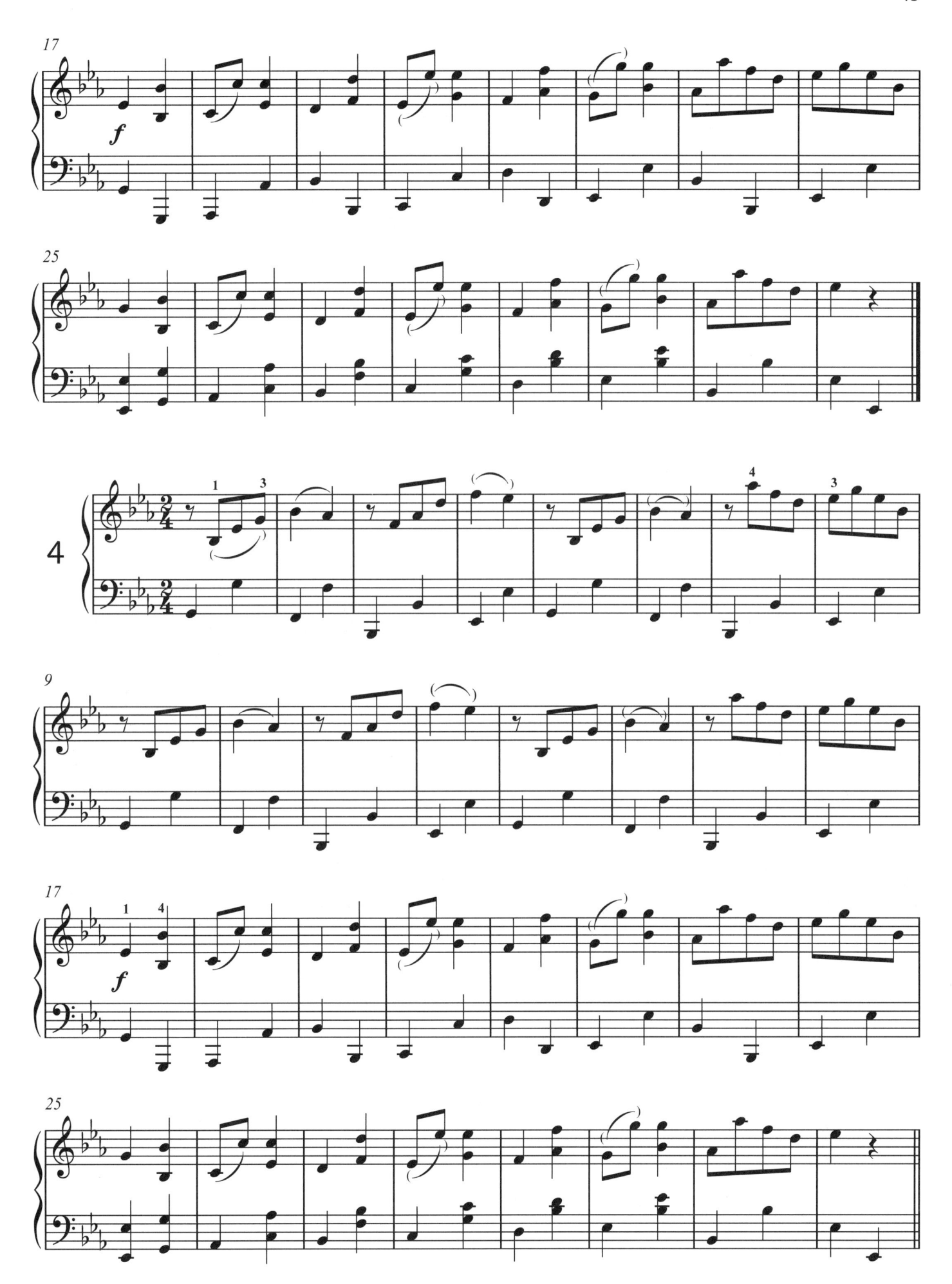

5

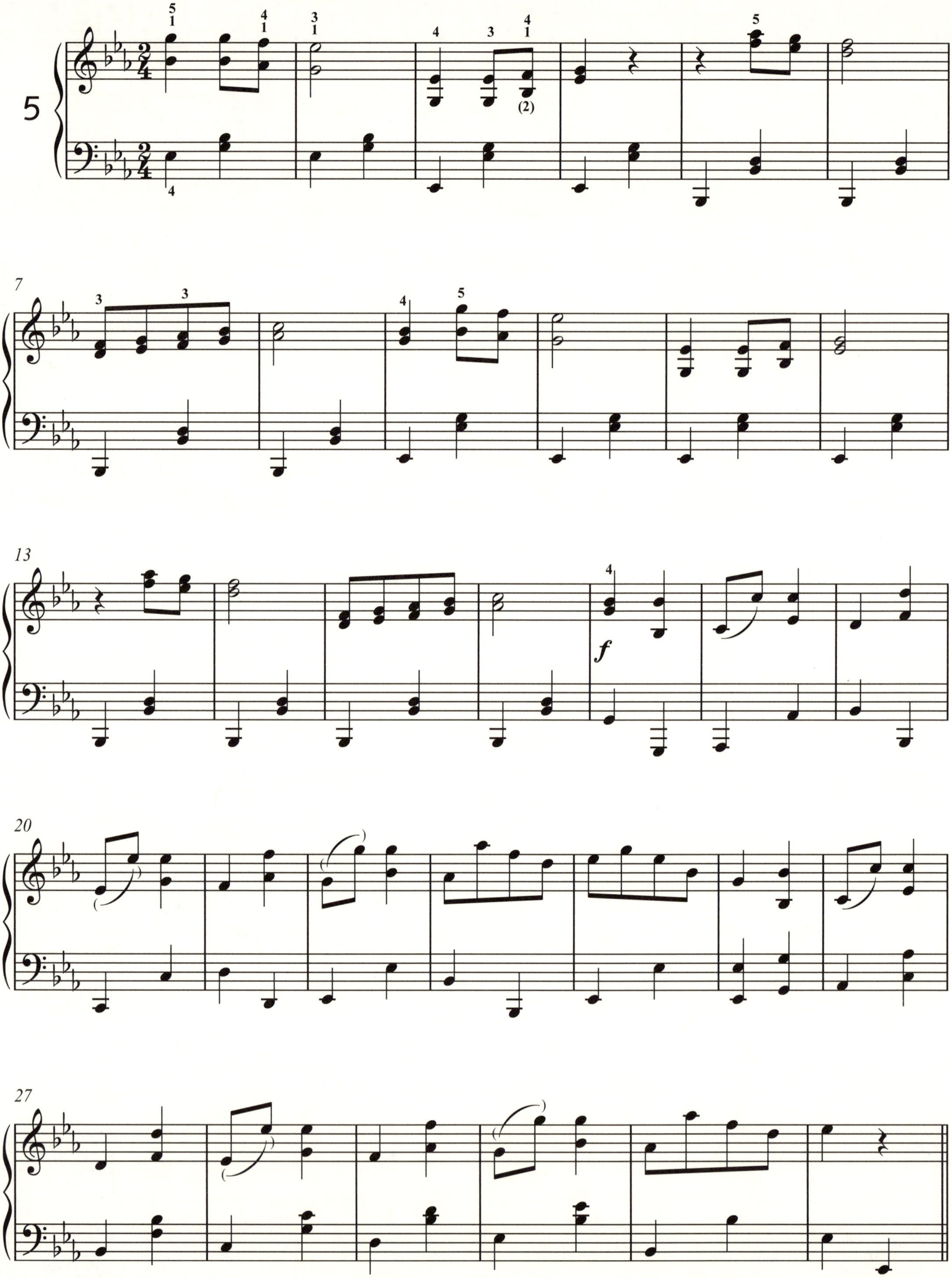

6

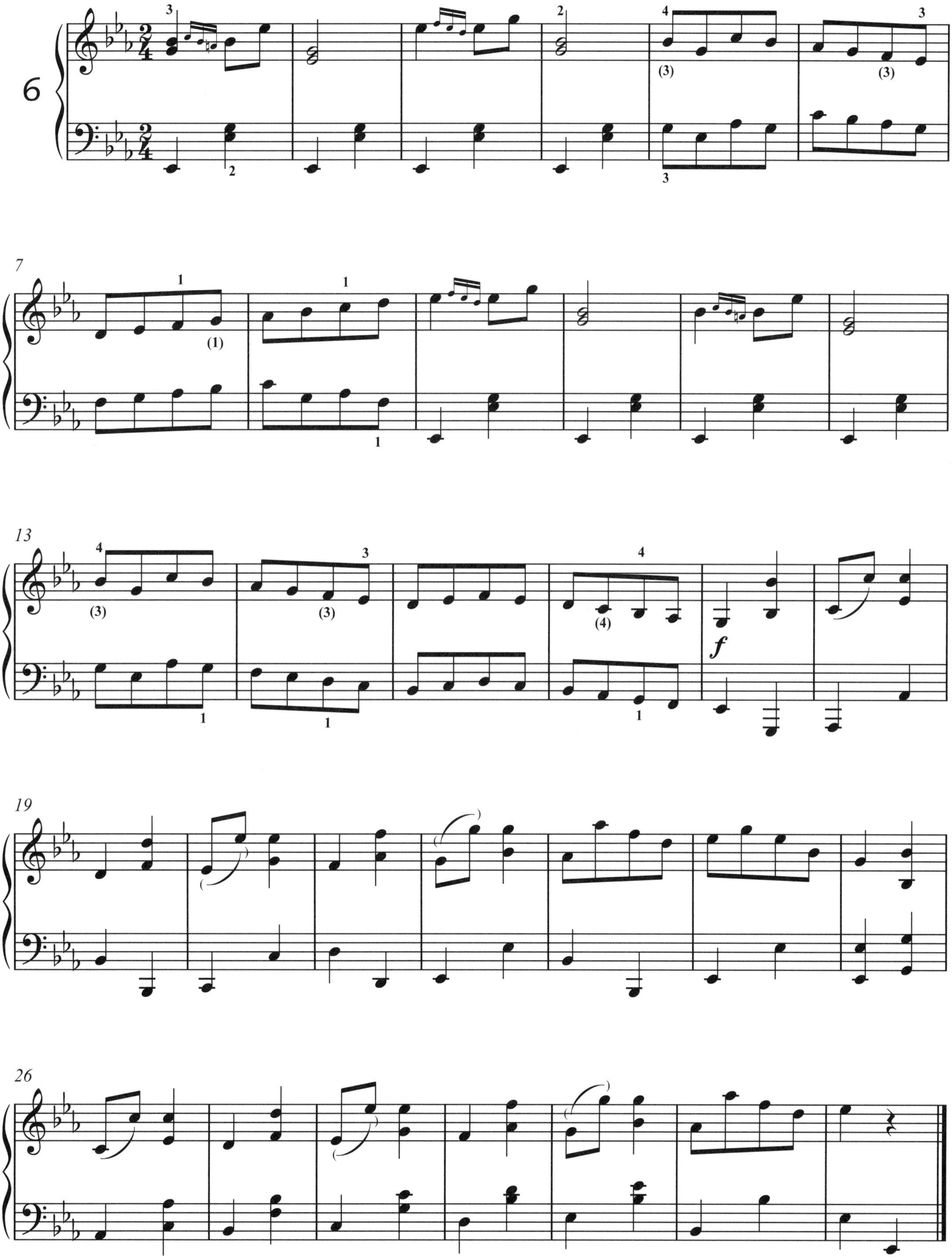

Bagatelle

D-Dur / D major
op. 33/6

Ludwig van Beethoven

Allegretto quasi Andante (♩ = 72)
Con una certa espressione parlante

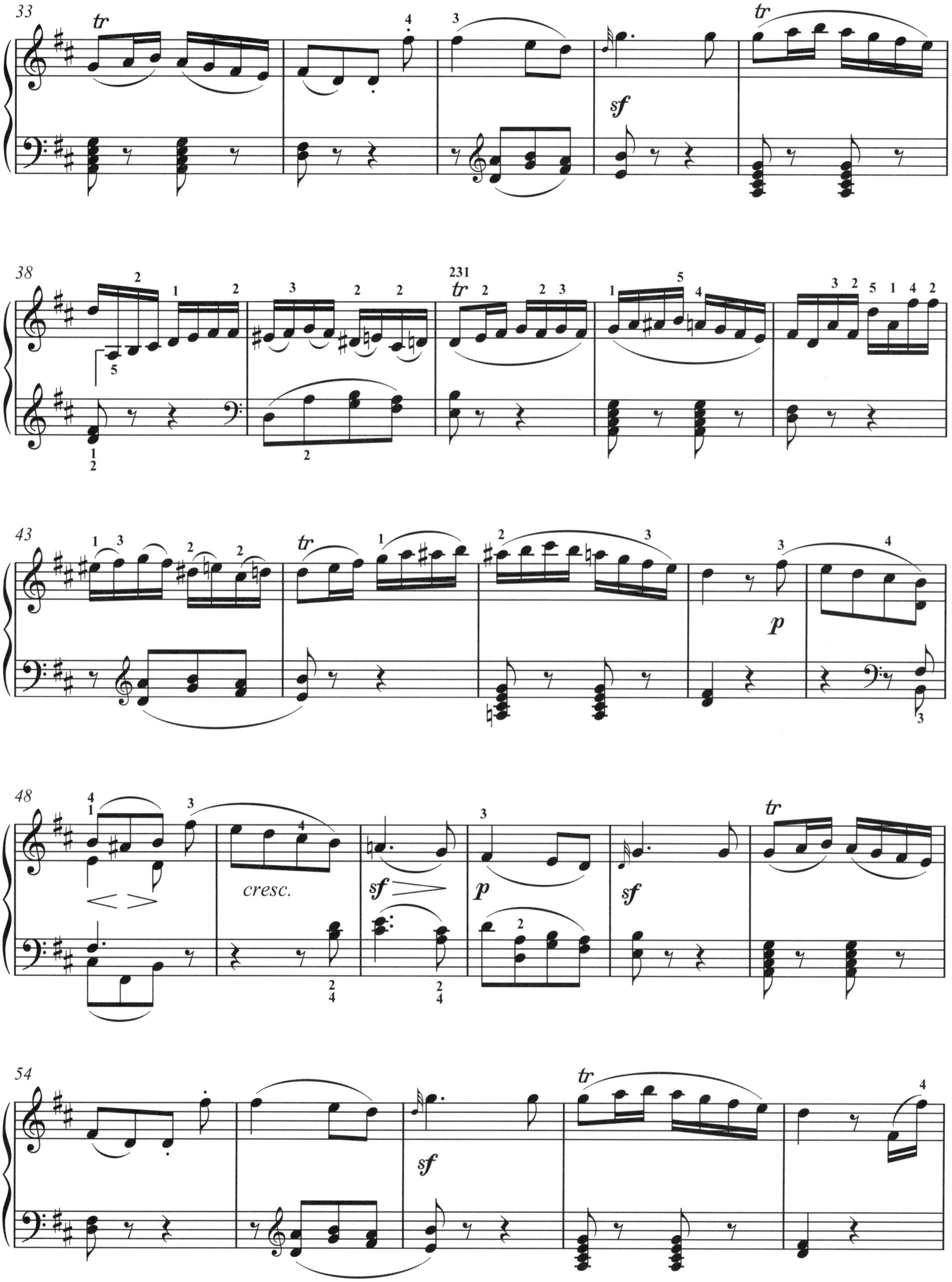
33
tr
sf
tr
38
tr
43
tr
p
48
cresc.
sf
p
sf
tr
54
sf
tr

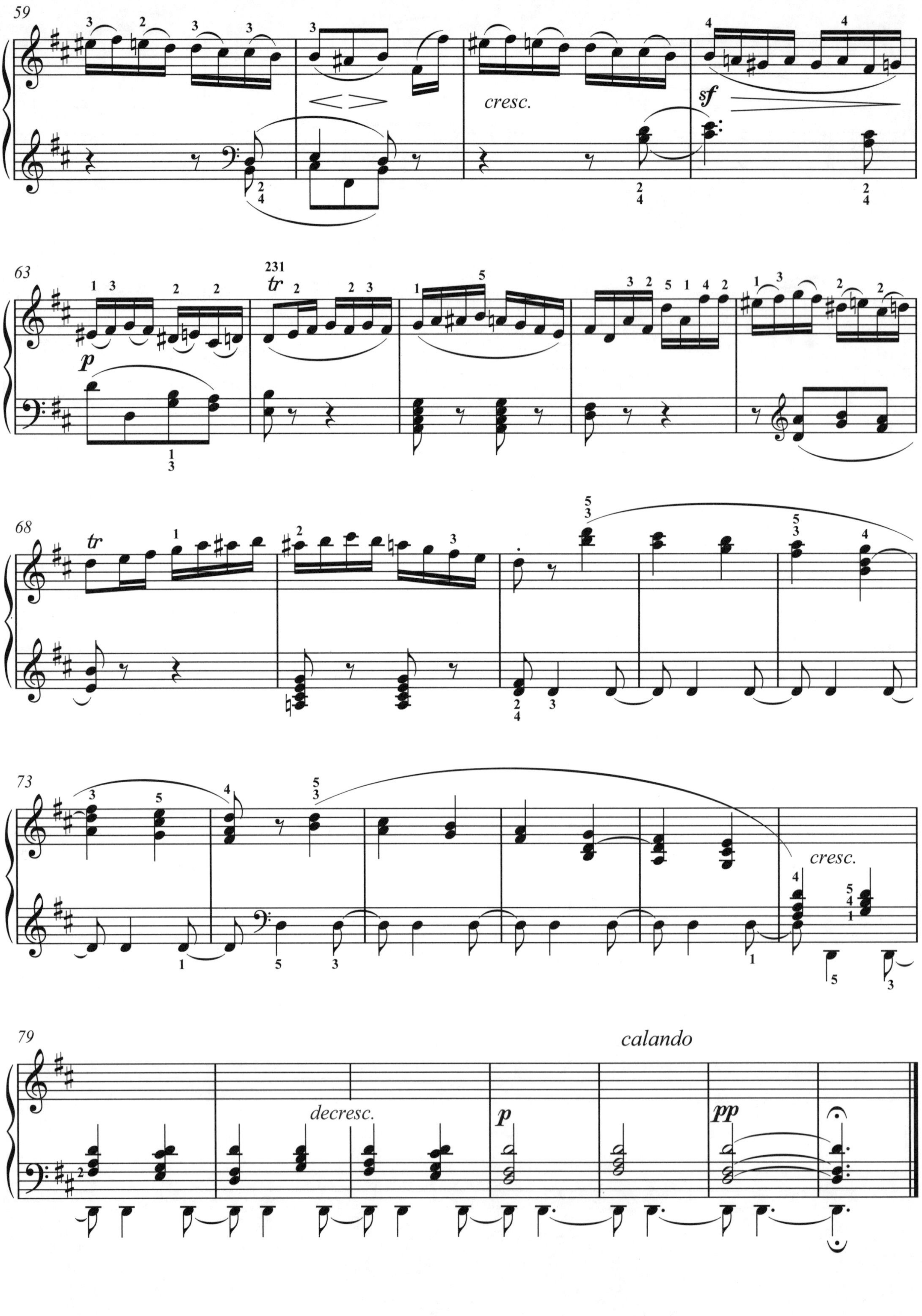
59
cresc.
sf
63
p
tr
68
tr
73
cresc.
79
calando
decresc.
p
pp

Bagatelle
g-Moll / G minor
op. 119/1

Ludwig van Beethoven

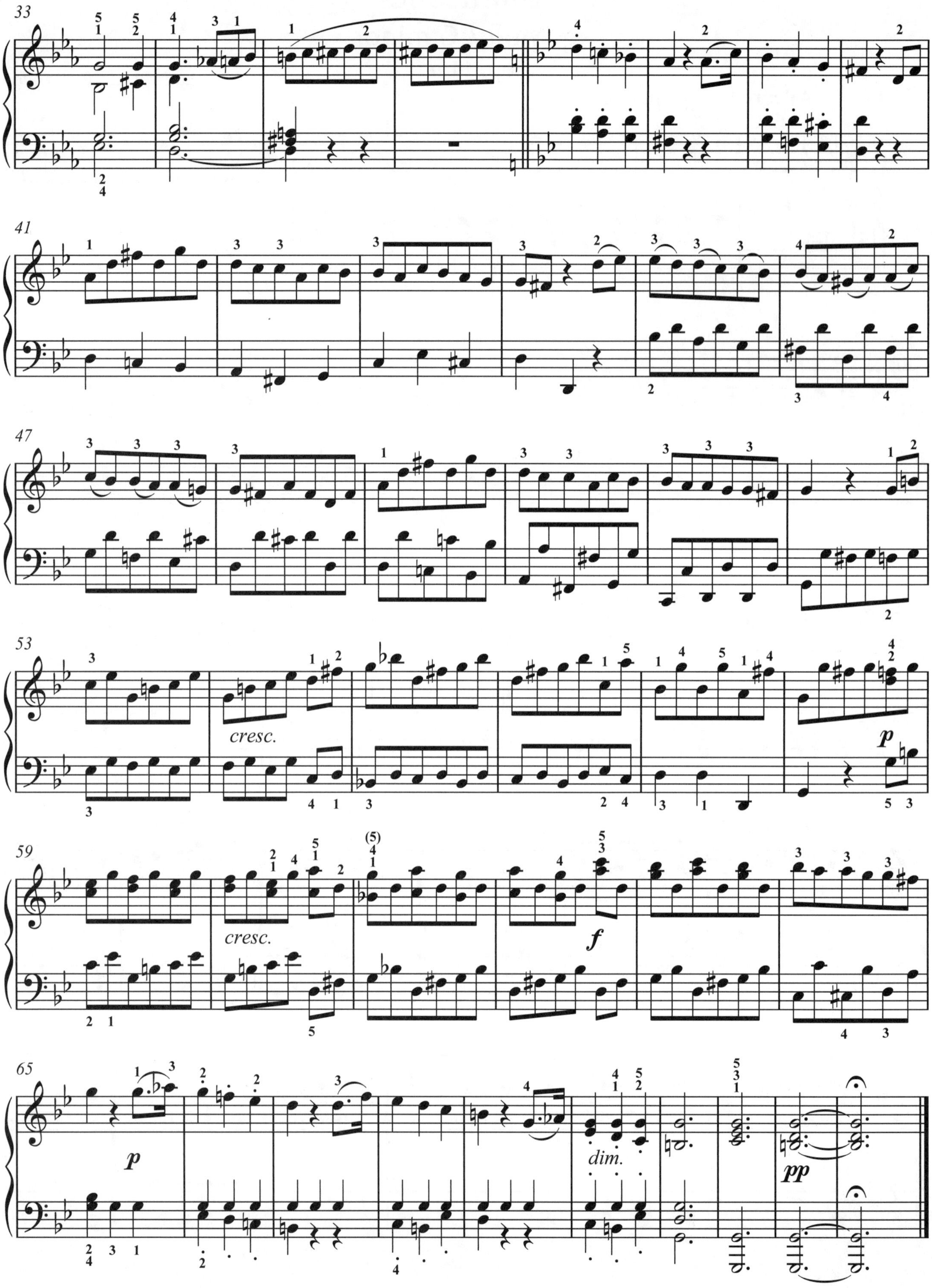
cresc.
p
cresc.
f
p
dim.
pp

Sechs Variationen / Six Variations*)
G-Dur / G major
WoO 70

Ludwig van Beethoven

Thema

(Andantino) (♩. = 56)

© 2016 Schott Music GmbH & Co. KG, Mainz

*) über / about "Nel cor più non mi sento", aus / from "La Molinara" von Paisiello
Vorschlag für eine leichtere Zusammenstellung: Thema, Var. I, Var. II, Var. IV, Var, III
For an easier compilation choose Theme, Var. I, Var. II, Var. IV, Var. III

Var. I

Var. II

Var. III

Var. IV

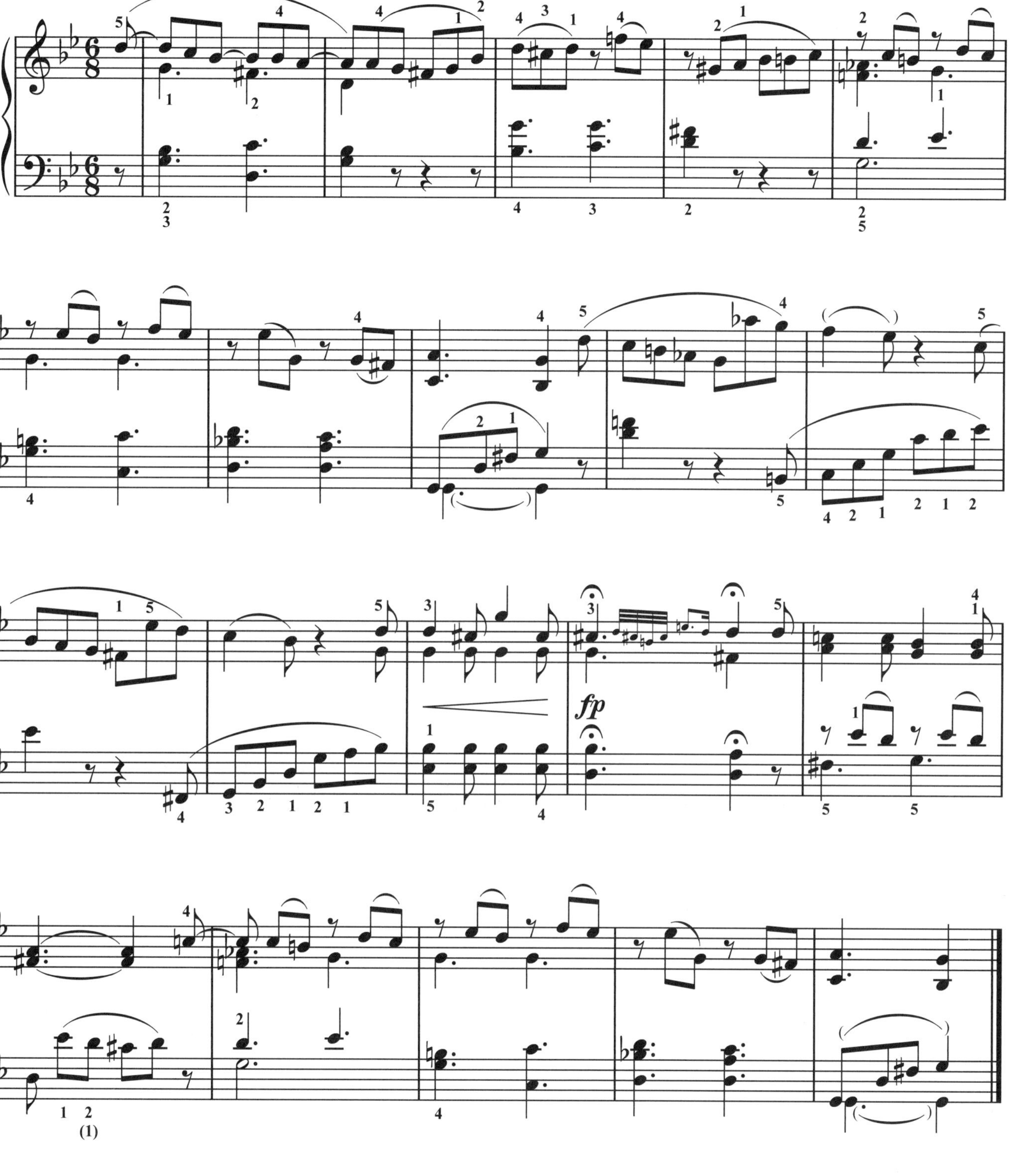

Var. V

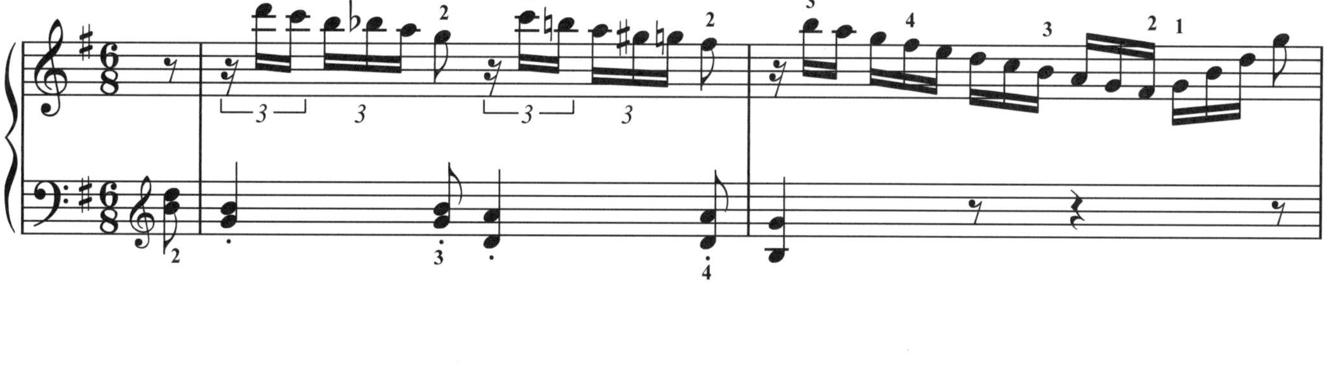

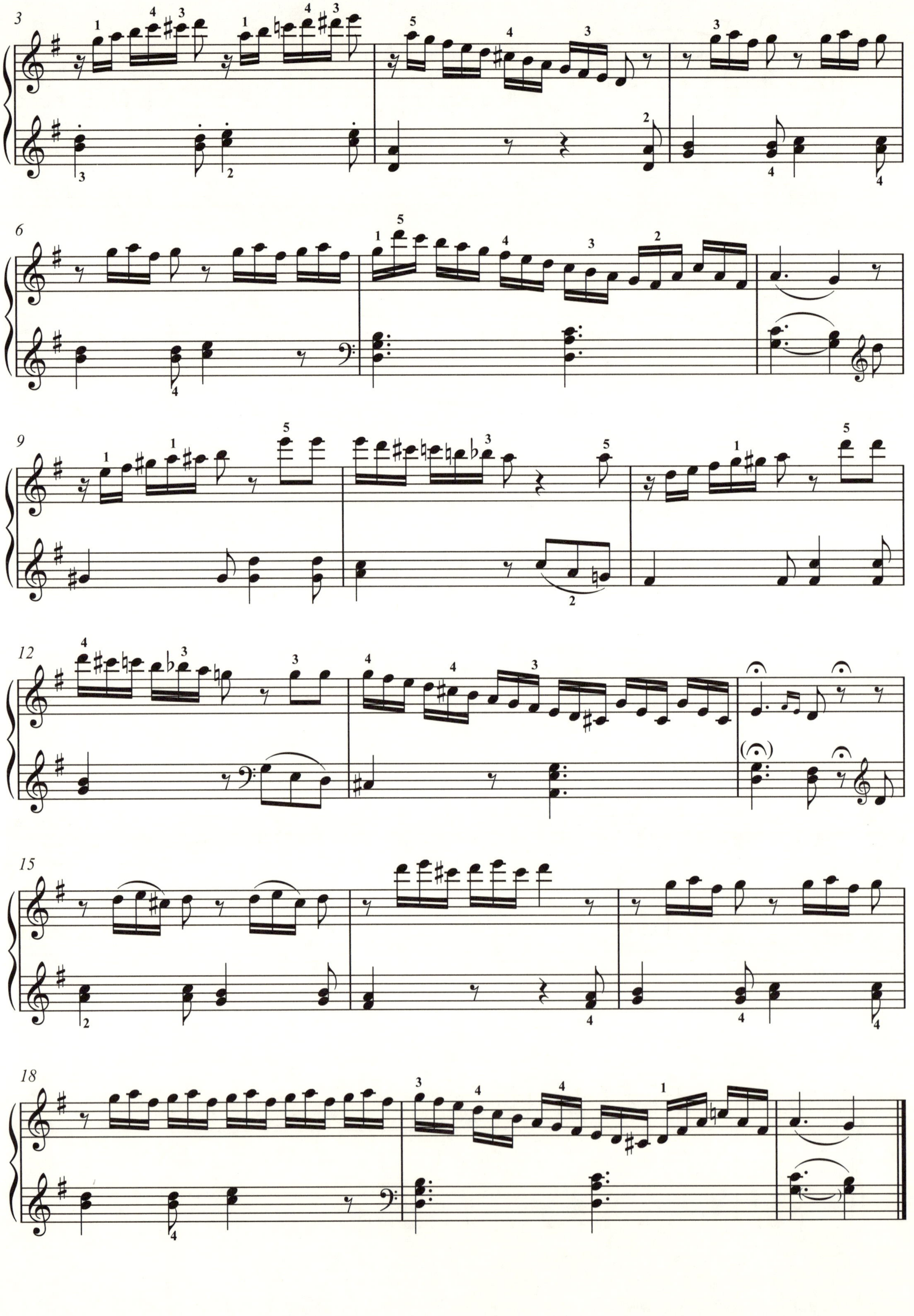

Var. VI

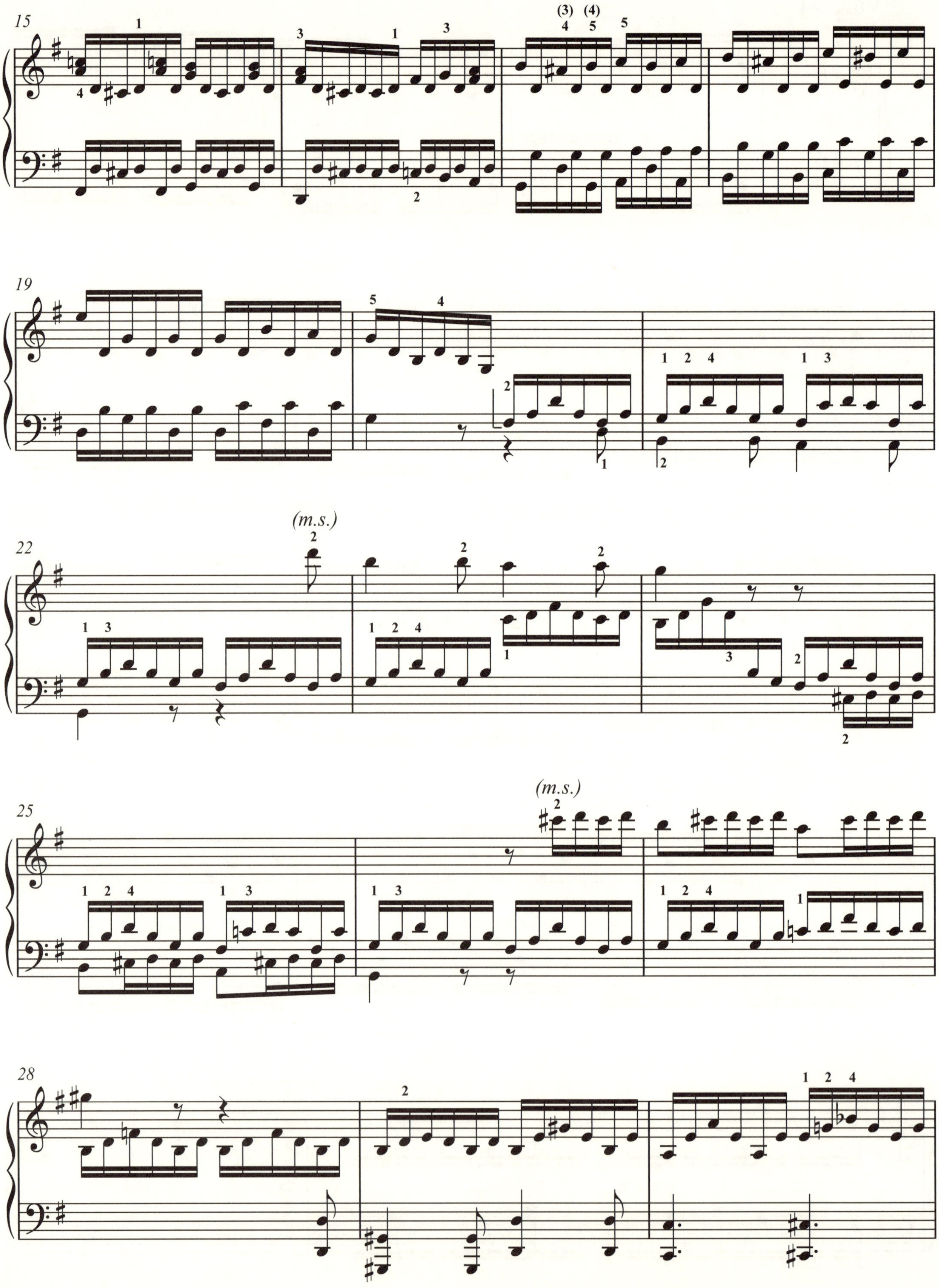
15
19
22
(m.s.)
25
(m.s.)
28

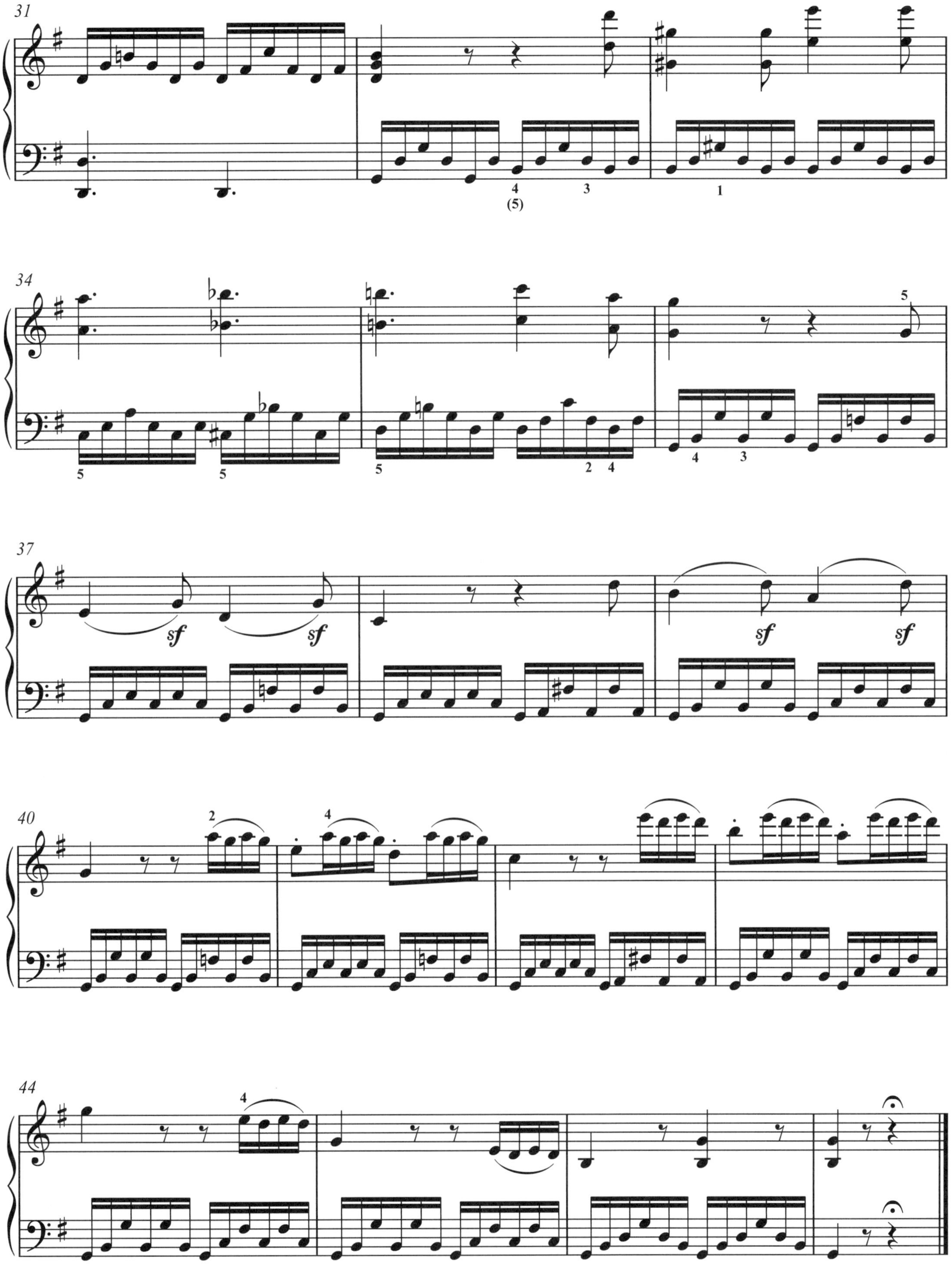
31
34
37
sf
sf
sf
sf
40
44

Mondscheinsonate / Moonlight Sonata
op. 27/2

I

Ludwig van Beethoven

Adagio sostenuto (♩ = 50 – 56)
Si deve suonare tutto questo pezzo delicatissimamente e senza sordini *)

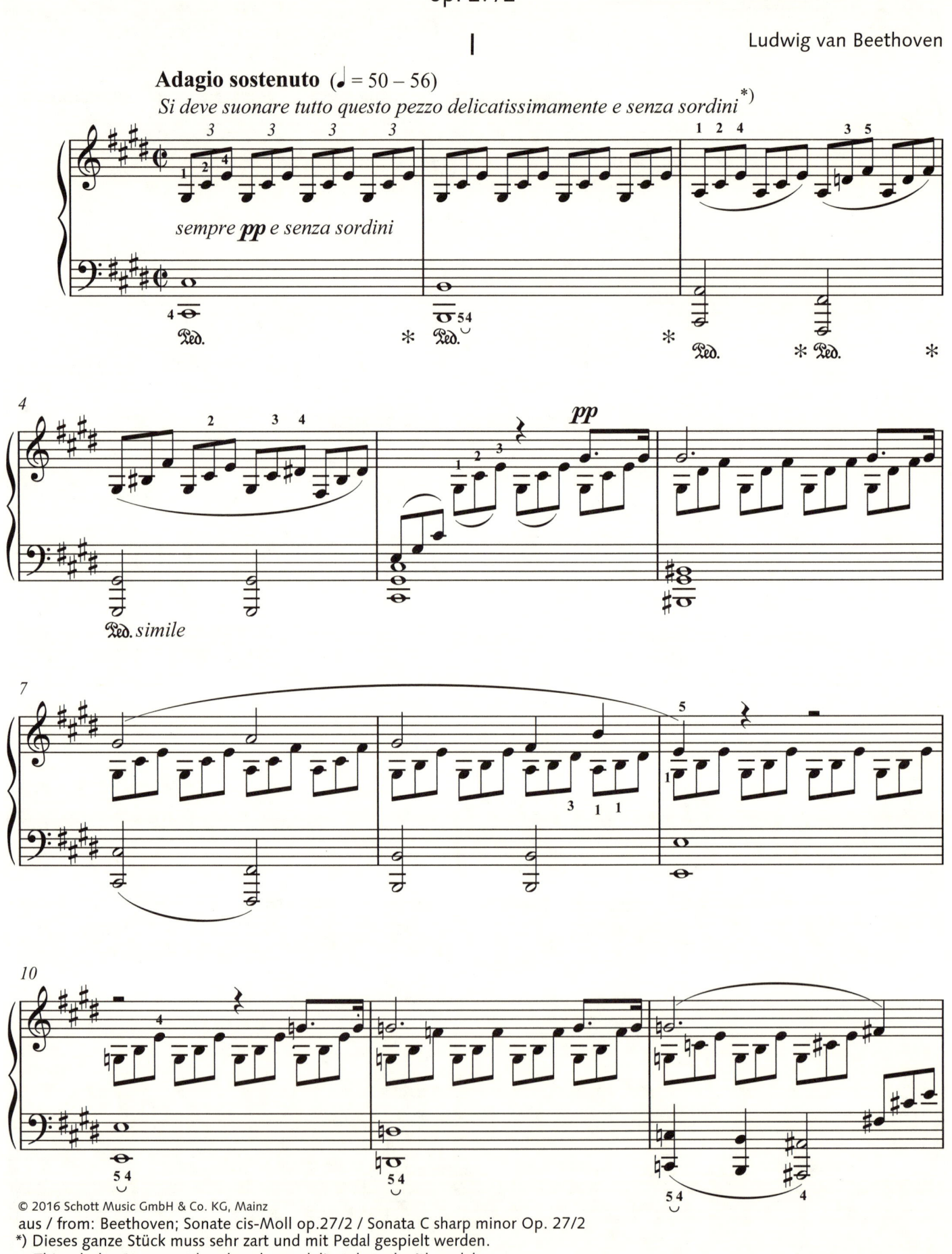

sempre **pp** *e senza sordini*

aus / from: Beethoven; Sonate cis-Moll op.27/2 / Sonata C sharp minor Op. 27/2
*) Dieses ganze Stück muss sehr zart und mit Pedal gespielt werden.
   This whole piece must be played very delicately and with pedal.

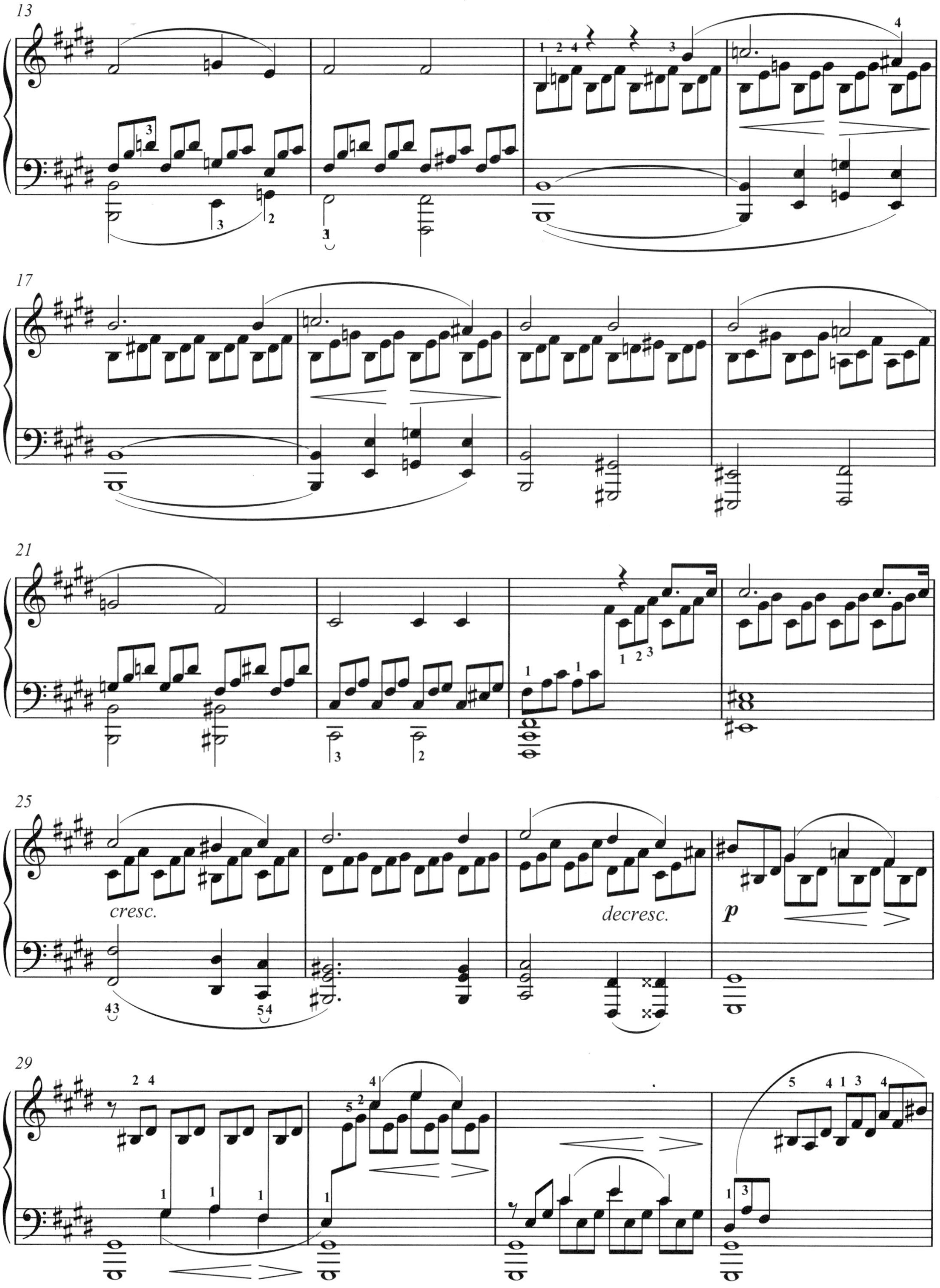
13
17
21
25
cresc.
decresc.
p
29

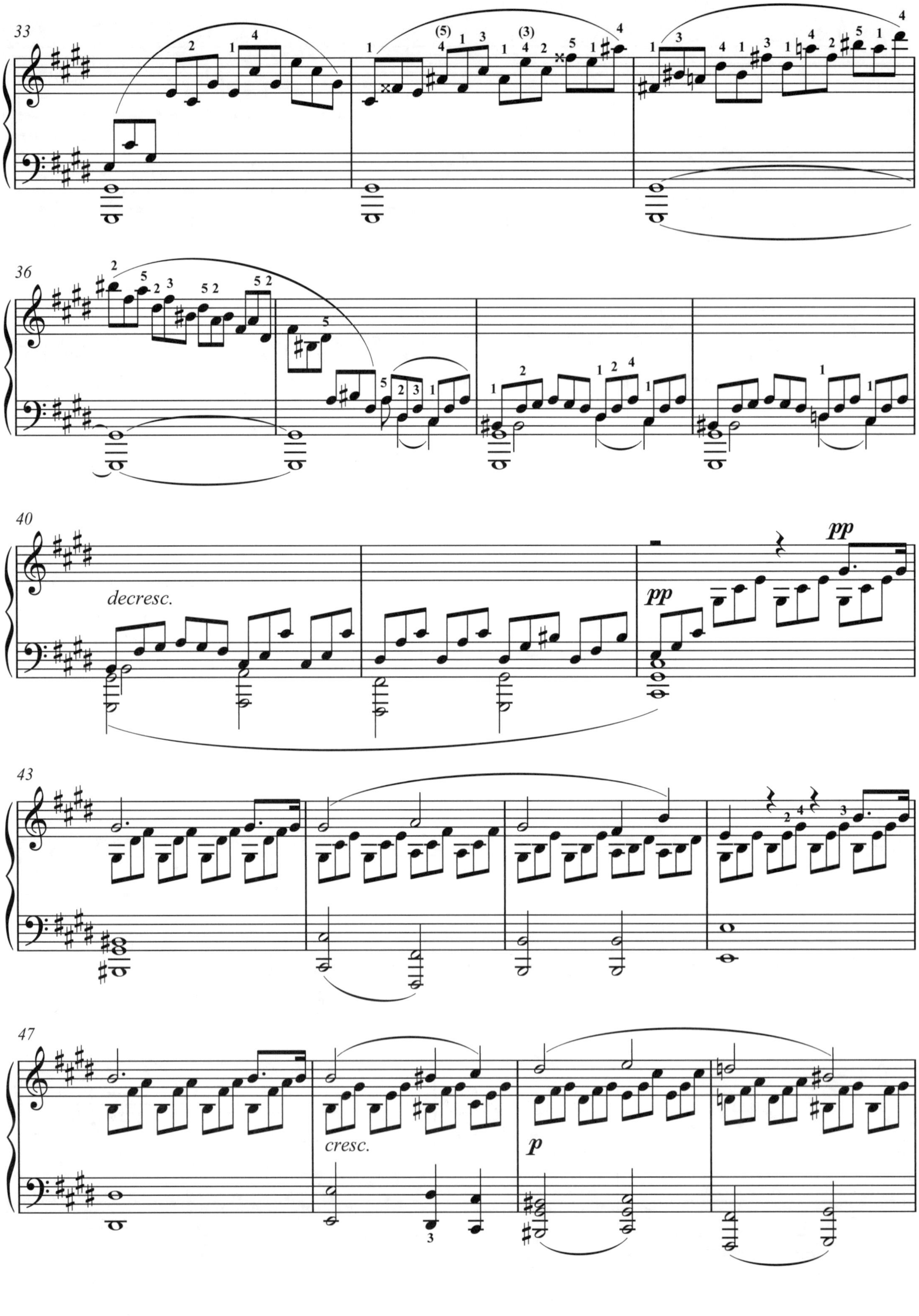
decresc.
pp
cresc.
p

*) für kleine Hände / for small hands